Gamification with Moodle

Use game elements in Moodle courses to build learner resilience and motivation

Natalie Denmeade

PUBLISHING

BIRMINGHAM - MUMBAI

Gamification with Moodle

First published: October 2015

Production reference: 1131015

Published by Packt Publishing Ltd.
Livery Place
35 Livery Street
Birmingham B3 2PB, UK.

ISBN 978-1-78217-307-6

www.packtpub.com

Credits

Author
Natalie Denmeade

Reviewers
Shashikant
Donald Schwartz

Commissioning Editor
Neil Alexander

Acquisition Editor
Nikhil Karkal

Content Development Editor
Siddhesh Salvi

Technical Editor
Tanmayee Patil

Copy Editors
Kausambhi Majumdar
Vikrant Phadke

Project Coordinator
Nidhi Joshi

Proofreader
Safis Editing

Indexer
Tejal Soni

Graphics
Jason Monteiro

Production Coordinator
Melwyn D'sa

Cover Work
Melwyn D'sa

Foreword

When I was "down under" recently for the KM Australia 2015 Conference in Melbourne, Natalie Denmeade and I met for coffee to explore areas of collaboration in the future. I was struck by Natalie's incredible passion for eLearning, applications of instructional technology, and most importantly, Gamification in the education process. Natalie has developed and demonstrated keen analytical capabilities, relationship building capacities, and a thirst for new knowledge that really impressed me. I have come across very few individuals who have her intellectual skills, leadership and team building drive, as well as her sensitive emotional intelligence.

My biggest surprise, once we began to talk, was Natalie's kind invitation for me to write the preface for her new book, *Gamification with Moodle*. I was exceptionally humbled. First, regardless of my grey hair and beard, I consider myself a Gamification apprentice—well, maybe more like a Sorcerer's Apprentice; but I think you get the idea. Second, Natalie has developed an incredible reputation in the Gamification field and the educational applications of gaming. Finally, Natalie is much more of a technical aficionado than I could ever be, especially with Learning Management Systems, such as Moodle.

Natalie has been working as a freelance educational Gamification consultant and Moodle administrator for many years. She has developed significant visibility as an educational transformation thought leader—what I would refer to as a disruptive "edupreneur". One of her publications, the *Moodle for Motivation Tool Guide*, has been distributed globally and translated into four languages. Natalie participates and leads many global communities-of-practice. Recently, her work included a project with Dev4X.com that will have a significant impact on villages where limited IT and Internet access is available.

Natalie has framed an exceptionally useful DIY approach to Gamification within the Moodle LMS. Her templates, advice, lessons, and learning strategies permit an instructor to experiment with direct application of Gamification techniques in any Moodle course. Such a rich knowledge repository of learning will dramatically reduce the amount of time and efforts required by an instructional designer to create a usable Moodle course. The performance increase for a Moodle-based instructor will be dramatic, and well worth the investment. However, her universal recommendations and framework can actually be embedded in many other LMSs. Instructors using Blackboard, CANVAS, Angel, or Desire2Learn, to name but a few LMSs, can benefit immensely from the applied and actionable knowledge contained in this text.

The application of Gamification within a Moodle course can create a significant experiential journey for both the learners and the instructor. Anyone reading this book has already gone over to the "dark side" and realized that in order to increase engagement, collaborative learning, and continuous learning, we need new, quicker, and agile approaches to embed Gamification mechanics and techniques within our courses.

We also respond better to micro-learning within an eLearning environment. Natalie's writing style and organization of the text facilitates an instructor's experience of gamifying a Moodle course, without overwhelming the teacher. Natalie's guidance throughout this book relies upon activities that are micro-learning-based, feature short-term lessons, projects, and coursework designed to provide the instructor with the chunking of the information and a scaffolding of the learning experience.

It has been my honor and privilege to be associated with Natalie's monograph filled with a wide range of "knowledge nuggets". Natalie has proved again that she is a critical thought leader in education and Gamification.

Michael J. D. Sutton, PhD
Wizened Ol' Fart, architect of experiential learning through Gamification, simulation, and serious games.
Boise, Idaho, USA, October 2015

About the Author

Natalie Denmeade works as a freelance educational Gamification consultant and Moodle administrator. She is interested in researching emerging technologies and how Gamification can transform traditional education. Her poster, *Moodle for Motivation Toolguide*, has been distributed widely as a useful tool to promote diversity in assessment. She has also developed an award-winning Moodle course using the Gamification design process. In 2015, she received a finalist certificate in the LearnX Impact Awards for instructional designer as a recognition of the high standards of her work. Through social media, Natalie participates in the global communities of mobile learning, Moodle Learning Management Systems, Gamification designers, and technology innovation groups.

Acknowledgement

This book is the result of collaborations of thousands of people actively involved in the global Moodle community, at www.moodle.org. Following the steps of other open source projects, educators around the globe now have a space to share ideas, write code, and support newcomers in the Moodle open source learning platform. Special thanks to Moodle HQ and the Moodle Partners (who are at the heart of this community). Feedback on the concept and text was graciously provided by Joyce Seitzinger, Donald Schwartz, Michael Sutton, Michael de Raadt, Bron Stuckey, Karrie Vitti, and Melanie Worrall.

www.moodle.org

Also, special thanks from Natalie to all of her students, who have given their permission to share their blogs and stories and have tolerated her testing and refining new ideas: "You have taught me a lot about games, play, and learning!"

About the Reviewers

Donald Schwartz has been designing, developing, deploying, and managing Moodle since 2003. He is an expert in video e-learning course presentation and delivery over CDNs to large and disparate clusters of Moodle sites. His clients have included medical societies, engineering schools, and a majority of the ENR top 50 for their CAD and BIM software training.

His other interest, besides fly fishing, is "wearable computing." Don leads the Wearables New England Meetup group and has facilitated hackathons, design sprints, and networking focused on wearables for healthcare in Boston and Washington DC.

Don is the principal of VectorSpect, LLC, (http://www.vectorspect.com), an e-learning consultancy based in New Hampshire, USA. Prior to striking out on his own, he spent 10 years developing and building the CAD learning, and e-learning networks for engineering and architectural designers.

Don previously technically reviewed *Moodle Administration Essentials*, *Packt Publishing* (https://www.packtpub.com/web-development/moodle-administration-essentials).

www.PacktPub.com

Support files, eBooks, discount offers, and more

For support files and downloads related to your book, please visit www.PacktPub.com.

Did you know that Packt offers eBook versions of every book published, with PDF and ePub files available? You can upgrade to the eBook version at www.PacktPub.com and as a print book customer, you are entitled to a discount on the eBook copy. Get in touch with us at service@packtpub.com for more details.

At www.PacktPub.com, you can also read a collection of free technical articles, sign up for a range of free newsletters and receive exclusive discounts and offers on Packt books and eBooks.

https://www2.packtpub.com/books/subscription/packtlib

Do you need instant solutions to your IT questions? PacktLib is Packt's online digital book library. Here, you can search, access, and read Packt's entire library of books.

Why subscribe?

- Fully searchable across every book published by Packt
- Copy and paste, print, and bookmark content
- On demand and accessible via a web browser

Free access for Packt account holders

If you have an account with Packt at www.PacktPub.com, you can use this to access PacktLib today and view 9 entirely free books. Simply use your login credentials for immediate access.

Table of Contents

Preface

This book describes how teachers can use Gamification design in their course development with the Moodle learning management system to build learner resilience and motivation.

Gamification is a design process that reframes goals to be more appealing and achievable using the principles of game design. The goal of this process is to keep learners engaged and motivated in a way that is not always present in traditional courses. When it is implemented through elegant solutions, learners may be unaware of the subtle game elements being used. A Gamification strategy can be considered successful if learners are more engaged and feel challenged and confident to keep progressing, which has implications for the way teachers consider their course evaluation processes. It is important to note that Gamification in education is more about how the person feels at certain points in their learning journey than about the end product, which may or may not, look like a *game*.

After following the tutorials in this book, teachers will gain the basic skills needed to get started with applying Gamification design techniques to their Moodle courses. They can take learners on a journey of risk, choice, surprise, delight, and transformation. Taking an activity and reframing it to be more appealing and achievable sounds like the job description of any teacher or coach. Therefore, many teachers are already doing this! Understanding games and play better can help teachers be more effective in using a wider range of game elements to aid retention and completion in their courses.

In this book, you will find hints and tips on how to apply proven strategies to Moodle course development, including the research on a *growth mindset* from Carol Dweck in her book *Mindset*. You will see how the use of game elements in Foursquare (badges), Twitter (likes), and LinkedIn (progress bar) can be applied to Moodle course design. You will use the core features available in Moodle. We will also explore new features and plugins that offer dozens of ways that teachers can use Moodle game elements such as, badges, labels, rubrics, group assignments, custom grading scales, forums, and conditional activities.

What this book covers

Chapter 1, Setting Up Gamification in a Moodle Course, shows you how to set up a scoring system using the Moodle gradebook. You use weekly categories to automatically add up scores for activities.

Chapter 2, Communication and Collaboration (Labels and Forums), explains how to establish a culture of collaboration in your class using Moodle forums. You will learn how to make use of activity loops that identify a kind of behavior and wrap motivation and feedback around that action.

Chapter 3, Challenges for Learners (Self-Assessment and Choice), helps you set challenges for learners to self-assess their current ability and set learning goals with the choice activity.

Chapter 4, Passing the Gateway (Conditional Activities), shows you how to configure gateways to check and ensure progress before new content or activities are released. These checks may be based on self-assessment, peer assessment, computer-based marking, or teacher grading.

Chapter 5, Feedback on Progress (Marking Guides and Scales), covers the setup of Moodle assignments and providing effective feedback through a comment bank and custom scales.

Chapter 6, Mastery Achieved (Badges and Motivation), illustrates how to issue open badges to recognize achievements and set up an online backpack to share digital badges.

Chapter 7, Leveling Up (Rubrics), helps you reduce anxiety for learners by using game-like *Leveling Up*. Through Moodle rubrics, learners can identify their current level and where they would like to be at a near point in the future.

Chapter 8, Completing the Quest (Reporting Activities), lets you quickly see who has read the instructions and completed tasks using Moodle automatic reports. These in-built analytics helps you identify and support those who need it the most.

Chapter 9, Super-boost Gamification with Social Elements (Groups), is where you discover how to increase motivation and participation by including social game elements in your Gamification strategies.

What you need for this book

You need access to your own test Moodle site using version 2.8 or later. The easiest way of doing this is by registering for a free Moodle Cloud site at www.moodle.com/cloud/.

Who this book is for

This book has been designed for teachers who use technology to create more engaging learning experiences for both online learning and face-to-face sessions. It will especially appeal to people who are interested in the underlying mechanics of playing and games and want to know more about applying these concepts in an educational context. It is assumed that you are a teacher and expert in your field, have basic computer skills, and have access to the Internet. If you have no previous knowledge of the Moodle Learning Management System (LMS) or Gamification, then this is a great place to start. The focus of this book is on why you would want to use each activity rather than detailed technical descriptions. Links to Moodle documentation with detailed instructions are provided throughout this book.

This book describes how to facilitate learning for groups of people who use the Moodle LMS. Moodle has become the world's leading software for teachers and workplace trainers. Although the examples used are for Moodle, the ideas can be used offline or with many other types of software or learning management systems. If you are only interested in Gamification in education and you don't use Moodle, then please keep reading and you will be able to adjust these ideas to your own preferred technology.

Conventions

In this book, you will find a number of text styles that distinguish between different kinds of information. Here are some examples of these styles and an explanation of their meaning.

New terms and **important words** are shown in bold. Words that you see on the screen, for example, in menus or dialog boxes, appear in the text like this: "Select **Edit profile** from the administration block to make changes."

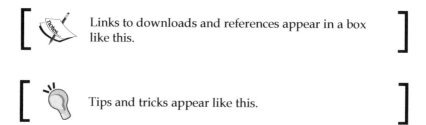

Links to downloads and references appear in a box like this.

Tips and tricks appear like this.

Reader feedback

Feedback from our readers is always welcome. Let us know what you think about this book—what you liked or disliked. Reader feedback is important for us as it helps us develop titles that you will really get the most out of.

To send us general feedback, e-mail `feedback@packtpub.com`, and mention the book's title in the subject of your message.

If there is a topic that you have expertise in and you are interested in either writing or contributing to a book, see our author guide at `www.packtpub.com/authors`.

Customer support

Now that you are the proud owner of a Packt book, we have a number of things to help you to get the most from your purchase.

Downloading the color images of this book

We also provide you with a PDF file that has color images of the screenshots/diagrams used in this book. The color images will help you better understand the changes in the output. You can download this file from `https://www.packtpub.com/sites/default/files/downloads/B04806_3076OS_Graphics.pdf`.

Errata

Although we have taken every care to ensure the accuracy of our content, mistakes do happen. If you find a mistake in one of our books—maybe a mistake in the text or the code—we would be grateful if you could report this to us. By doing so, you can save other readers from frustration and help us improve subsequent versions of this book. If you find any errata, please report them by visiting http://www.packtpub. com/submit-errata, selecting your book, clicking on the **Errata Submission Form** link, and entering the details of your errata. Once your errata are verified, your submission will be accepted and the errata will be uploaded to our website or added to any list of existing errata under the Errata section of that title.

To view the previously submitted errata, go to https://www.packtpub.com/books/ content/support and enter the name of the book in the search field. The required information will appear under the **Errata** section.

Piracy

Piracy of copyrighted material on the Internet is an ongoing problem across all media. At Packt, we take the protection of our copyright and licenses very seriously. If you come across any illegal copies of our works in any form on the Internet, please provide us with the location address or website name immediately so that we can pursue a remedy.

Please contact us at copyright@packtpub.com with a link to the suspected pirated material.

We appreciate your help in protecting our authors and our ability to bring you valuable content.

eBooks, discount offers, and more

Did you know that Packt offers eBook versions of every book published, with PDF and ePub files available? You can upgrade to the eBook version at www.PacktPub. com and as a print book customer, you are entitled to a discount on the eBook copy. Get in touch with us at customercare@packtpub.com for more details.

At www.PacktPub.com, you can also read a collection of free technical articles, sign up for a range of free newsletters, and receive exclusive discounts and offers on Packt books and eBooks.

Questions

If you have a problem with any aspect of this book, you can contact us at
questions@packtpub.com, and we will do our best to address the problem.

1
Setting Up Gamification in a Moodle Course

Gamification in education is a design process that reframes goals to be more appealing and achievable by tapping in to our emotions. From a game designer's perspective, *fun* is just another word for learning. Once we have figured out the patterns in a game, it stops being fun. The challenge is to learn how to play it.

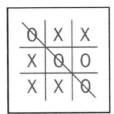

Figure 1.1: The Book 'Theory of Fun' by Raph Koster describes people as, 'amazing pattern matching machines'

Games create resilience in players by creating a series of adequate challenges that are satisfying to resolve. Sid Meier says: *Games are a series of interesting choices.* Jane McGonigal stresses how important emotions are throughout this learning journey:

> *Game Designers are obsessed with emotion. How do we create the emotions that we want gamers to feel, and how can we really make it this intense, emotional experience?*

This book offers both pedagogical and technical guidance on applying game-thinking to education. Follow the step-by-step guide to create a very basic course that acts as a framework ready for your own content. Firstly, and most importantly, this approach is ideal for busy teachers and encourages creativity, ownership, and the ability to respond to the changing needs and situations in the classroom. Secondly, this approach keeps learners more engaged and creates opportunities for motivation through status, access, power, and stuff, which, as described by Gabe Zichermann, are the basics of Gamification. Professor Dweck's research has shown that a *growth mindset* is what creates resilience. Through the book you will see how game designers have achieved this very well and how teachers can use these ideas in course design.

Moodle for motivation poster

This book presents an in-depth look at the principles of Gamification with Moodle, as outlined in this poster published by Natalie Denmeade in 2013, *Moodle for Motivation* (see the following figure):

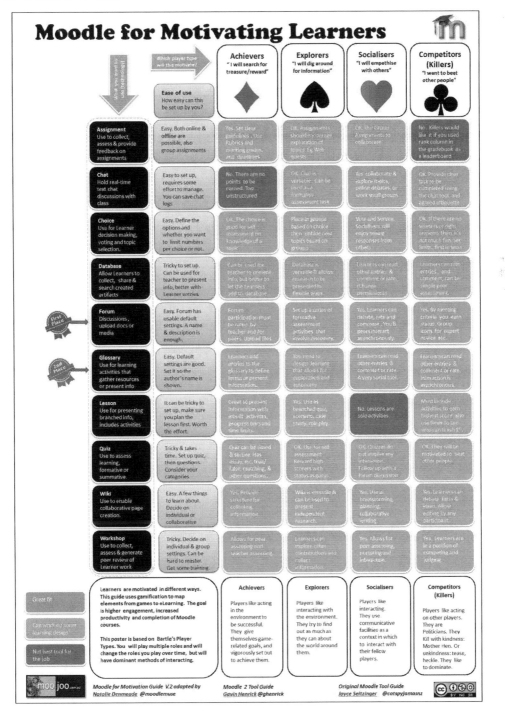

Figure 1.2

This poster can be downloaded from

www.bit.ly/mfm2013

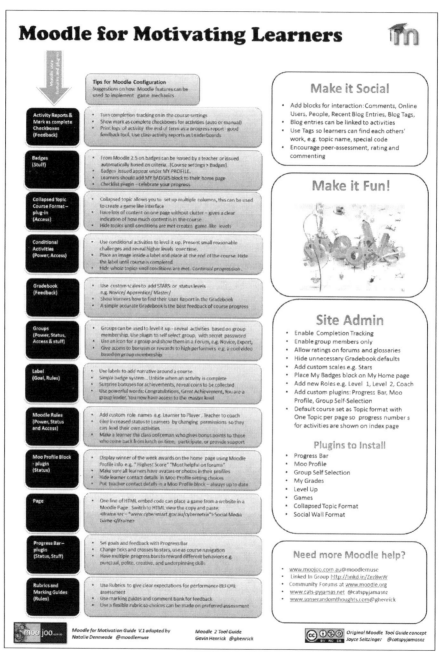

Figure 1.3: Moodle for Motivating Learners

Standardized outcomes yet personalized delivery

Standardized outcomes do not require standardized delivery. Technology should give teachers more choices and the freedom to teach the way that feels right to them and reduces their workload. Teaching from a pre-made course can feel restrictive and can take away the fun and responsiveness of being a teacher. In this book, you will learn a progressive development approach to create a Moodle Course that does not assume that everything will be set up before day one of the course. You will set up a framework, which can be filled in with detailed activities over time. Most teachers start with a series of learning outcomes but do not have the time available to plan every assessment and activity for the entire semester. Even if they did, they would miss out on including current news and events, encouraging learner-inspired projects, and responding to the skills and interests of the new batch of learners.

You could use a pre-assembled Gamification platform, such as Badgeville or Classcraft. This system may have a shorter learning curve and may be easier to set up than a blank Moodle Course. However, like any software wizard, you will become frustrated when you are locked in a system you can't alter, or the changes you require can only be made site-wide instead of at the course/class level. In some circumstances, pre-made Gamification software would meet your needs. However, this book presents Moodle as being a worthy technology to explore the range of game elements available for you to assemble in any order that you need. Moodle is already the world's most popular learning management system globally used in 225 countries with 68 million users. You are invited to contribute extension code or ideas to this successful open source project to keep it evolving.

In my experience, Moodle is the most versatile Gamification platform for education. Teachers can reduce their administration load, increase learner completion rates, and make the process more fun and rewarding for both themselves and their learners. As you try out each activity, you will see how the social constructionist pedagogy underlying Moodle — that we learn by doing, collaborating, and communicating — is closely aligned to game design principles. If you want to become a master of Gamification and continue to teach in your own style, then, in my opinion, Moodle is the best Gamification platform to invest your time in learning.

Watch a video on introduction to Gamification in education by Natalie Denmeade (one hour) at

`https://www.youtube.com/watch?v=02nHOIZY7V0`

Objectives

This book covers the following three objectives:

- Understanding the Gamification design process
- Freeing up time to be creative
- Identifying learner progress and providing personalized learning paths

Understanding the Gamification design process

You will learn how to use game elements in Moodle to take learners on a journey of risk, choice, surprise, delight, and ultimately, transformation, and how to create courses that appeal to a diverse range of learners. We will discuss how learners require different types of feedback as they progress through the learning journey. The goal of this feedback is not only to reward and acknowledge mastery of the current task, but also to do the following from Jeff Sandefer's, The Learner Driven Revolution:

> *"empower people to take ownership for their learning, contribute to a learning community where people learn to set goals, self-organize, and grow as competent and confident people with a deepening sense of agency"*

Minecraft has achieved this for a whole generation of children who haven't yet learned to read or write. As educators, we can borrow ideas from video game designers (who borrowed ideas from an ancient line of entertainers and storytellers) to motivate and engage people to complete their learning journey.

Freeing up time to be creative

You will learn how to configure Moodle activities to reduce repetitive administration tasks such as checking whether work has been completed by all the learners, ensuring that the required documents have been received, or meeting audit reporting requirements. The challenge is to use computers to do the repetitive tasks that eat up your time and leave the creative rewarding aspects of teaching to you. You don't have to automate everything, so you are not expected to know how to use every activity in Moodle, rather you will start with what you find comfortable and effective in your context. Once you are convinced that this has really saved your time and that the process has been enjoyable, then you will be challenged to add another activity to your repertoire. In fact, you only have to master three activities to get to the end of this book! You really don't have to learn it all before you jump in and try. You wouldn't expect this from your learners and we don't expect this from you. Trust your instincts! You will know this works when you feel the change in the vibe of the room, or in the after-hours voluntary activities, or the increase in peer-mentoring, and more joy for both you and your learners.

Identifying learner progress and providing personalized learning paths

The full power of placing learning activities within an LMS is that the sequence can create a personalized learning path. Technology in education is often under-utilized as a simple repository of files, when it can be so much more. The Moodle activities you create will automatically create data on learner participation and competence to assist you in identifying struggling learners and plan appropriate intervention/scaffolding. Activities for advanced learners can be revealed according to the criteria you set. The in-built reports available in Moodle LMS not only help you to get to know your learners faster, but also create evidence for formative assessment.

Setting up a test environment

A free online Moodle sandpit is available for you to try out the suggestions at `http://school.demo.moodle.net/`. Log in with the `Teacher` username and the `Moodle` password. The Mount Orange Demo site is reset every 60 minutes and will always use the latest release of Moodle software that will be similar to the older versions but has extended features.

Alternatively, you could download a free copy of Moodle to test on your own computer from `https://download.moodle.org/releases/latest/`. You should be able to follow most of the steps in this guide with any version of Moodle 2.x (2.1, 2.2, and so on).

Register for your own free fully functional Moodle Site at `www.Moodle.com/cloud`

For advanced users, extensions to the Moodle core package can be installed directly or downloaded from `https://moodle.org/plugins/`. Bitnami offers free cloud hosting for a test Moodle site and local install packages for download at `https://bitnami.com/stack/moodle`.

Recommended plug-ins for Gamification are included in this book at the end of each chapter.

You are guided how to create your own Moodle course throughout this book. A finished version is available for download at `www.OpenEducationBadges.com`.

Further training in Gamification is provided on this site, and you are invited to join the learning community to find support and inspiration as you get started.

Setting up scoring in your test course

Allow ten minutes for this activity:

Add categories to the Moodle gradebook expand and collapse columns in the gradebook.

The Moodle gradebook is often a last thought, which is a shame because it is one of the most powerful ways of showing progress on a learning journey. It takes ten minutes to set up the gradebook to tally weekly scores of XP and/or reputation points. You will need access to a test Moodle site and your own test course, as discussed in the introduction, to follow these steps.

1. Go to **Administration | Course administration | Edit settings**.
2. Choose **Weekly format**, if you don't have the time to set individual dates on each activity. You can reuse this next semester without changing the dates.
3. Choose four (or more) weeks to follow this step-by-step guide.
4. Change the **Course layout** to **Show one section per page** to keep a minimal design:

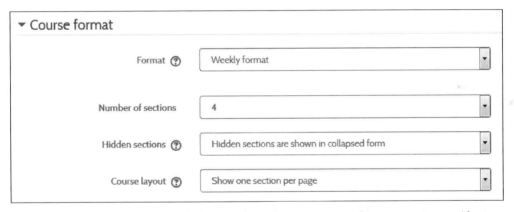

Figure 1.4: Weekly format is great for busy teachers who want to re-use this course next year without changing dates

Adding gradebook categories

Take a few minutes to set up categories in your gradebook as the first step to keep scores throughout your course:

1. In the **ADMINISTRATION** block of your course, select **Grades**.

2. By default, you will see **Grader report**. Use the drop-down box (or possibly tabs in your site) to select **Categories and items.** See the following screenshot:

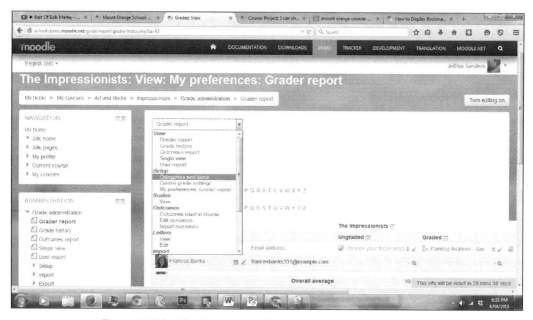

Figure 1.5: Select the 'Categories and items' to add and mange categories

3. The demo course shown in the following screenshots has two categories set up: **Graded** and **Ungraded**, which is a great start that any course should use as a minimum requirement. In your own test course, add these two top level categories of **Graded** and **Ungraded**. Use the button at the bottom of the page to *Add category*.

4. We are going to go a few steps further and add subcategories under **Graded** for at least four weeks. Use the button at the bottom of the page to *Add category*. Ensure you select a parent category for **Graded**.

The parent category will calculate the total in a variety of ways. At first, you should keep it as simple as possible with the **Natural** default option (older versions of Moodle call this *Sum of Grade*). Moodle 2.8 hides advanced options. Even so, the options are endless and can be overwhelming. For now, keep with the simplest approach until you face a need for a different calculation.

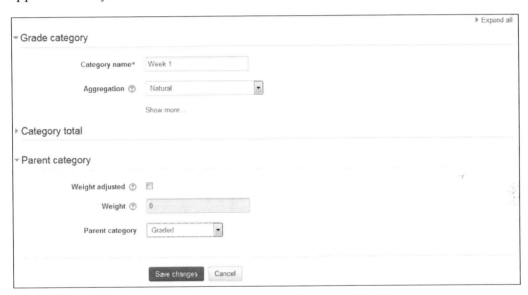

Figure 1.6: Set up a category for Week 1 and another for Week 2 and so on

Switch views back to your **Grader report** using the drop-down menu. Notice that each week can be collapsed or expanded to see weekly tallies of points earned, for example, **Week 4 total** (see the following screenshot):

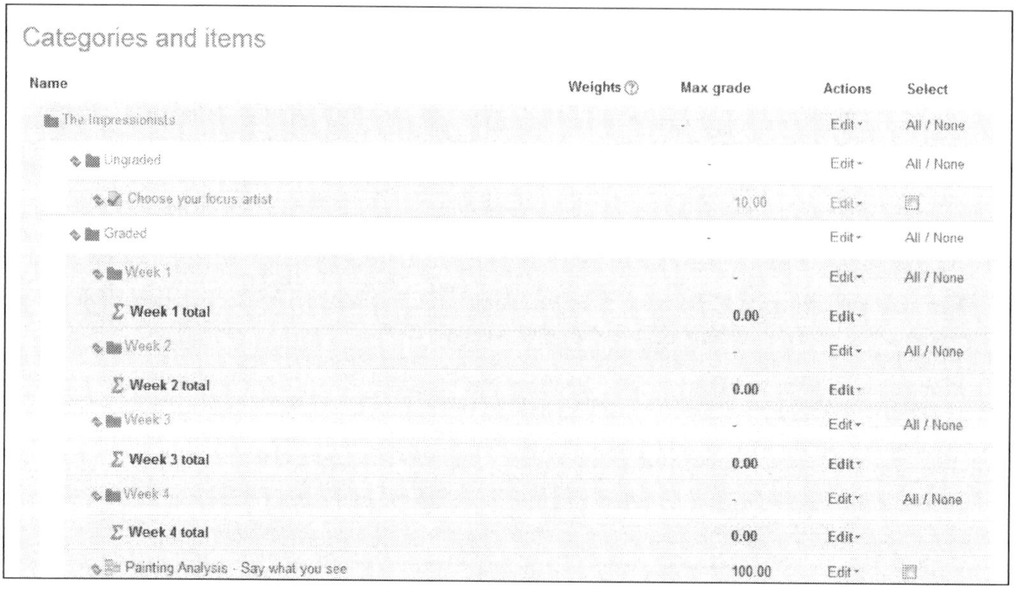

Name	Weights ⑦	Max grade	Actions	Select
■ The Impressionists	-		Edit ▾	All / None
◆ ■ Ungraded		-	Edit ▾	All / None
◆ ☑ Choose your focus artist		10.00	Edit ▾	☐
◆ ■ Graded		-	Edit ▾	All / None
◆ ■ Week 1		-	Edit ▾	All / None
Σ Week 1 total		0.00	Edit ▾	
◆ ■ Week 2		-	Edit ▾	All / None
Σ Week 2 total		0.00	Edit ▾	
◆ ■ Week 3		-	Edit ▾	All / None
Σ Week 3 total		0.00	Edit ▾	
◆ ■ Week 4		-	Edit ▾	All / None
Σ Week 4 total		0.00	Edit ▾	
◆ ■ Painting Analysis - Say what you see		100.00	Edit ▾	☐

Figure 1.7: Add categories to your gradebook for each week so that you can tally the weekly scores automatically

From now on when you create an activity, you can place it in these pre-defined categories:

Velvet Throne [–]								
Week 1	Week 2	Week 3	Week 4	Week 5	Week 6	Week 7		
Wk 1 Total	Wk 2 Total	Wk 3 Total	Wk 4 Total	Wk 5 Total	Wk 6	Cup of Fate Achievements	Velvet Throne Participation	Best fire breathing dragon
105	27	58	100	0	28	–	20	–
95	16	54	0	0	19	–	20	–
8	23	–	100	0	10	–	20	–
0	23	–	0	0	23	–	20	–
80	24	27	0	0	24	–	20	10

Figure 1.8: Each weekly total can be expanded or collapsed using the + sign next to the heading

When you create new activities, you will be able to choose which grading subcategory they should be placed in. At the very least, having activities in the two categories of **Graded** and **Ungraded** makes the gradebook more accurate for learners. We will place a few activities within each *week*. This is a flexible approach because you can have any number of activities within a *week* and use the gradebook as a calculator. It also allows you to back up the whole course and reuse it next year with a weekly session plan starting from your chosen date. Also, this way you don't have to change due dates on assignments and quizzes each term.

The first time you attempt this in your class, you may prefer to use paper or a simple spreadsheet over a three-week test run to build your own confidence in the process.

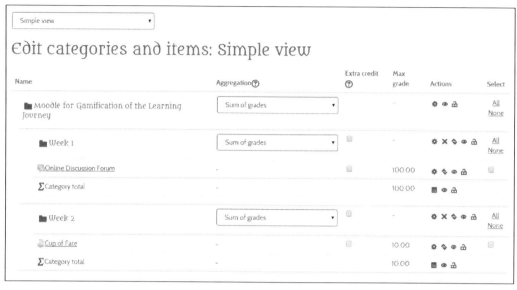

Figure 1.9: In the versions prior to Moodle 2.8, choose **Simple view** to add the categories. Change the total to **Sum of grades**. In Moodle 2.8, this is called *Natural* scoring

 When starting to use these calculations, choose **percentages** in the gradebook view to help in seeing how the calculations are being made. For example, **Grade display type** default **(percentage)**, so you will see results such as **45 (90%)**.

Figure 1.10: Show both the real value and percentage in the gradebook while you are planning your course scoring system

Read more about the Gradebook on Moodle Docs at
`https://docs.moodle.org/28/en/Grader_report`

Summary

In this chapter, we used the Moodle gradebook to organize groups of activities into categories. Earlier versions of Moodle offered many options to cater to the different needs of schools around the globe. Moodle 2.8 offers a much simpler interface and layout. From now on, every activity can be placed in the correct category on creation. This will save you time and make your gradebook more accurate.

Keeping the gradebook accurate makes it easier for your learners to get a clear feedback on progress. Hide any elements you don't need by clicking on the little eye icon. You can hide the course total completely, if it is misleading in the final result. Students can access course grades by a link in the **ADMINISTRATION** block. If you don't need to use the gradebook, then use the Moodle course settings page and change the gradebook to be not displayed.

The next chapter will inspire you to start thinking like a game designer when you start adding activities in your Moodle course. There are simple and quick changes you can make that will have a powerful effect on learner engagement.

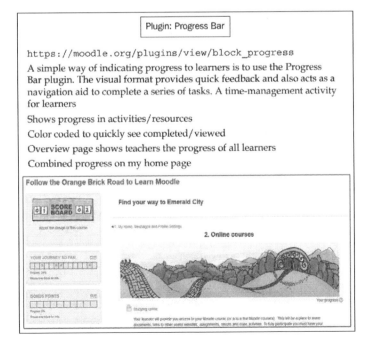

2
Communication and Collaboration (Labels and Forums)

This chapter is about establishing a culture of communication and collaboration in your class as a learning community. You will learn to use Moodle labels in inventive ways to mimic games and set up a Moodle forum for peer interaction.

The time allotted will be 30 minutes to set up a forum and some labels in your course.

This chapter will cover the following topics:

- Activity loops and onboarding experiences
- The importance of ownership and choice in creating an identity
- Establishing a culture of communication and collaboration

Mount Orange demo Moodle site

It is best to follow these steps in your own test Moodle course that you will set up on www.moodle.com. As an example, we will refer to the demonstration course on Mount Orange School at http://school.demo.moodle.net/course/view.php?id=63:

1. Go to http://school.demo.moodle.net/login/index.php.
2. Log in to this free test site with the teacher username and moodle password.

3. Take a note of the message in the bottom right corner that states the number of minutes until the site is automatically reset (maximum of 60 minutes). Any change that you make will be wiped at this point, so play away—you can't break it!

Figure 2.1: The preceding screenshot is of a free demonstration site to experiment with Moodle LMS using the fictional "Mount Orange School"

You are now logged in to this test Moodle site as **Jeffrey Sanders**, a teacher at a fictional place called Mount Orange School. From the **My home** page, find the course "The Impressionists" that we will use as a demonstration course.

The quickest way to find this page again is to use your bookmarks bar. Highlight the web address for this course and drag it to the bookmarks bar. This is a great tip to tell your learners. If they are signed in to the browser with a Gmail account, their bookmarks will be synchronized to help them in finding your Moodle course (and other online learning spaces), whether they are at school, home, or work (see the following figure).

Figure 2.2: The top-right image in the screenshot indicates that I am signed in with my Gmail account. This will keep the bookmarks of my eLearning sites that I can easily access from any computer

Profiles and avatars

Select the name **Jeffrey Sanders** (in the top-right corner) and view **My profile**. Imagine this from a new learner's point of view. First impressions are very strong. Do you feel that you know Jeffrey Sanders from the image he chose? What information is missing from this page? The profile page in Moodle is an important way for learners to get to know each other and find out how to contact each other.

Select **Edit profile** from the administration block to make changes. The first activity that a new person needs to do, when they start a Moodle course, is to update their profile. It is not necessary to explain everything to the learners, but here are a few important things to demonstrate:

- Make sure that their e-mail addresses are current, so that they receive notifications of new messages.

- Explain the privacy options to show or hide their e-mail addresses, and use nicknames for their online personas rather than real names. The city can be entered as Anonymous where appropriate.

- Explain the subscription choices and how they can manage e-mail updates.

- Encourage the learners to enter their interests, so that they can connect to other people and use these as conversation starters.

- Upload a profile picture or an avatar.

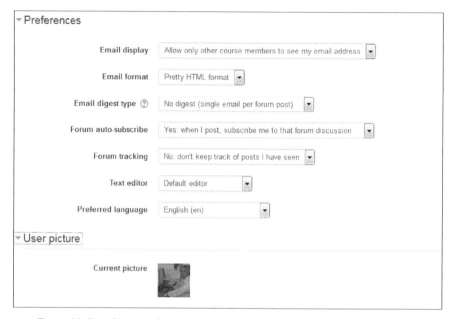

Figure 2.3: Spend time explaining the Moodle profile setting and privacy options to new learners

Messaging and forums

In the administration block, go to **Messages**. Ask learners to look for your current course in the contacts list. Ask them to send a welcome message to you explaining how they found out about this course and what they want to achieve. They should also send a brief welcome message to two other learners who have similar interests. Explain to them that they can create a "contacts list" and block anyone if necessary. You may wish to negotiate some boundaries around online communication and review your school's online etiquette and anti-bullying policies. Try this in "The Impressionists" course where you can find test users contacts for practice.

Taking the time to guide the learners through the creation and upload of an avatar is a crucial step towards making them feel welcome in this new environment and having some ownership. Watch how long children spend in dressing up their avatar in the games. It brings them joy and power to choose how they are represented. A creative way to do this, in Moodle, is to ask the learners to use themes such as "superheroes" or Lego characters while choosing a profile image. There is a free website to create a Lego avatar at `http://sigfigcreator.thelegomovie.com/`. Or perhaps they can choose an animal to represent themselves? It is even better if you can relate it to your course content. In this course, on "The Impressionists", you could ask the learners to choose their favorite painting as their avatar.

Activity loops

Game designers use the activity loops of **Motivations**, **Action**, and **Feedback**. This holds people accountable for an action. Instead of just asking people to create and upload an avatar and hoping they would do it, you could incorporate this in a series of activities. Set up a forum and make a post to invite people to reply with a **Hello** message. Each person has to select another learner's name to view their profile, and then rate each other's avatars by rating the forum post out of 3. First, let them rate your avatar so that they know how this works.

This completes the activity loop as you have provided them with three things: motivation to participate, a clearly defined action, and peer-generated feedback.

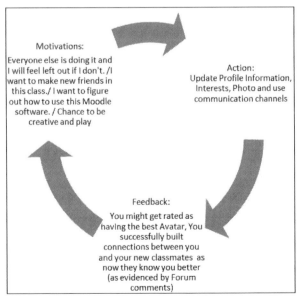

Figure 2.5: Every action can be mapped to multiple motivations

To set up a forum in a Moodle course, you need to add an activity as follows:

1. In your test course, turn on the editing mode using the button on the top-right corner.

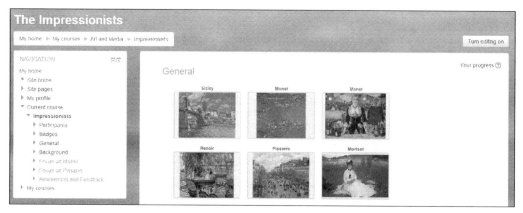

Figure 2.6: Turn on editing to allow teachers to add and edit content in a Moodle course

2. Select **Add an activity or resource** in the bottom-right corner of the first section and choose **Forum**.

3. Enter a name and description of the forum.

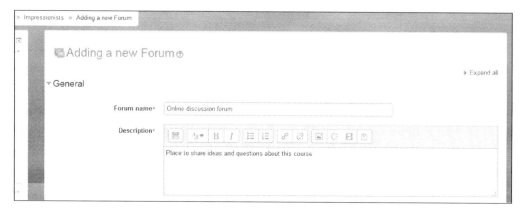

Figure 2.7: Add a new forum to your course

4. Choose a **Grade category** of **Week 1** for the scores from this forum to be recorded.

5. Choose a rating of a score of 3 points. Each rating will be calculated as an average score of 1-3 (see the following screenshot):

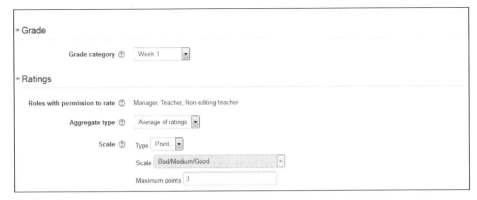

Figure 2.8: Set up the ratings on the forum posts

6. By default, only you have the right to rate the forum posts but you can change this. In the **ADMINISTRATION** block, go to **Forum administration | Permissions**. Scroll down until you see **Rate posts**. Select the **+** sign to add the "students" who will now be able rate the forum posts. This will take a few minutes for you, but think how much time you will save by outsourcing to students. Try this in the Mount Orange demo course first if you are nervous about changing permissions. See the following screenshot:

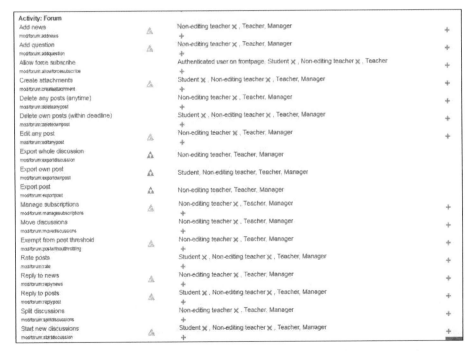

Figure 2.9: You can lighten your workload by adding students who are permitted to "rate posts"

Figure 2.10: The box to rate forum posts automatically appears for teachers, but you can add the permissions for learners as well to rate the posts

Figure 2.11: Administer forum settings to add permissions for learners to the rate posts

Forum moderation

You have control over moderating comments made on this forum. Although it is a risk to ask learners to rate each other's work, having negotiated the agreed online etiquette you will be surprised how motivating this is for your group. Like Facebook has aptly demonstrated, tapping in to our need for affiliation is a very powerful force. Your learners will be generally fair in their assessments of each other. Feedback from peers is experienced differently than feedback from a teacher. Try this—you will be surprised what a good vibe this will create! If you didn't attempt a face-to-face lesson because there might be behavior issues to address, you probably wouldn't be a teacher. In an online environment, there will be a few tricky situations to navigate. However, the potential benefits of setting up communication lines and collaboration make this worthwhile. Each event is a learning experience.

Watch this slideshare presentation by Vinnie Stocker on 101 ways to use an online forum:

`http://www.slideshare.net/vinnystocker/101-creative-ideas-for-forums-13091996`

ally out of 1-3 by setting the maximum score in
rsions of Moodle have other options to rate on a
other social media websites.

cale. In the gradebook, select **Scales** and at the
le". Moodle 2.8 now allows single rating scales
n Moodle.org forums. Read this next sentence
ore first. For example, D, C, B, A as scales are
adebook. Note that there is no comma at the
they are a type of font that you won't find on
TML stars from a webpage to Moodle. Try
d add it to your test course. You can then select
a **Grade category**, or for the overall course total.

ol, Fairly cool, Cool, Very cool, The coolest

A list of the HTML symbols can be found at http://www.
w3schools.com/charsets/ref_utf_symbols.asp
Read more on the Custom Scales Moodle Docs at
https://docs.moodle.org/28/en/Scales

Onboarding

Game designers create onboarding experiences that ease new players through
a welcoming/training experience. The time you spend taking learners through
creating avatars and then using a forum to compare the results may seem like a
waste of time, if it is not directly linked to academic performance. However, you
could view this process as an "onboarding experience". The creator of *Plants vs.
Zombies* offered this advice on how to subtly introduce people to a new game
interface in his presentation at the **Games Developers Conference** (GDC):

Blend the tutorial into the game:

- Better to have the player "do" than "read"
- Spread out the teaching of game mechanics
- Just get the player to do it once
- Use fewer words (eight words on a screen is the optimum!)
- Use unobtrusive messaging if possible
- Use adaptive messaging
- Don't create noise
- Use visuals to teach
- Leverage what people already know

 Watch a webinar on providing tutorials and help by a leading game designer at `http://gdcvault.com/play/1015541/How-I-Got-My-Mom`

At this point in your Moodle course, you need to be very specific about the minimum amount of information a learner needs to get started. Now would be a bad time to explain how to submit assignments or other Moodling skills that they do not need yet. Schedule your tutorials throughout your course and provide no-risk practice versions of a Moodle activity before the "real event" to reduce anxiety.

Have a look at a few courses on the Moodle Mount Orange demo site and ask yourself these questions. How can you introduce tutorial information at the right time (just in time), rather than at the beginning (just in case)? How can you design the first interactions with a Moodle course to be enjoyable? How can you set up the equivalent of onboarding activities that teach learners how to use each activity in Moodle? How can you reduce the available options to make it very clear and fail-safe that the expected choice is made? How can icons and graphics be used to make instructions clearer? Can Moodle create adaptive messaging to suit learner levels? What can you do about the people who do want to read all the instructions first?

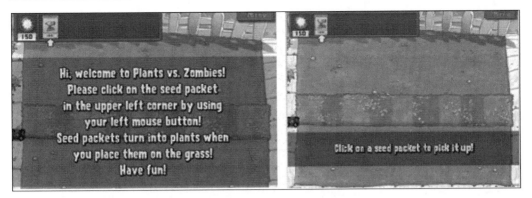

Figure 12: Option A or B? Online Instruction needs to be succinct and direct. Being polite and explaining details is clutter

Moodle labels as tutorials

Moodle labels are an effective way of placing text or images on a Moodle page. When adding instructional text, it is tempting to write the words as you would speak in a classroom. Game designers avoid any unnecessary words and details on the screen. Although this may seem abrupt, it is far more effective in an online environment as seen in the preceding two examples of *Plants vs. Zombies*. To add a label turn editing on, select **+Add activity or resource**, and choose **Label**.

Game designers know that once players are involved in a game they are ready to soak up the tutorial information. In the first few minutes, the objective is to make the game enticing and fun and to build up trust between the player and the system. As players progress, they face challenges and receive hints when they fail. This approach allows the joy of discovery. If you design this in reverse and tell people what they need to know first, then they don't feel smart when they figure it out. Providing too much instruction on how to face a challenge is damaging to the trust built up between the player and the system.

Summary

In this chapter, we started developing the onboarding phase. The sequence proposed is designed to achieve multiple goals such as encouraging learners to upload a profile picture and create their online persona, inviting learners to look at each other's profiles and speed up the process of getting to know each other, introducing learners to the idea of forum posting and rating in a low-risk (non-assessable) way, taking the workload off teachers to assess each entry, and enforcing compliance through software options that saves the teacher's time and creates an expectation of work standards for learners.

We used an activity loop that identifies a behavior and wraps motivation and feedback around that action.

Now you have learnt the importance of avatars and profiles in creating an online identity. You have seen how a basic forum can be used to involve learners in peer assessment. You are now ready to start setting up challenges that build resilience. In the next chapter, we will borrow ideas from game designers on how to use risk, choice, and uncertain rewards to maintain interest throughout the learning journey.

Plugin: Moo Profile

Moodle can display a teacher's or a learner's profile as a block on your course page using the Moo Profile plugin. You could change this regularly in the first few weeks to help people to get to know each other's names. The block can be customized to include an unlimited number of users' profiles, a custom block title, and an optional summary. You can display or hide any user profile data:

Show if a user is currently online or not

Show a link to send a message

Show the profile(s) of the course teacher(s)

Show the profile of a quiz marker and link to support

Show the profile of a winner of a competition or a highest achieve

---

3

Challenges for Learners (Self-Assessment and Choice)

This chapter is about using the Moodle assignment to record scores for offline (face-to-face) activities. You will also see how the simple Choice activity can be used for self-assessment.

This chapter will cover the following topics:

- Self-assessment
- Score keeping
- Growth mindsets
- Suspense and risk
- Uncertain rewards and dopamine

Moodle assignments

The most popular activity used in Moodle is the assignment activity that is mostly used to upload a document for grading. With some creative thinking, you can implement many game elements with this simple activity:

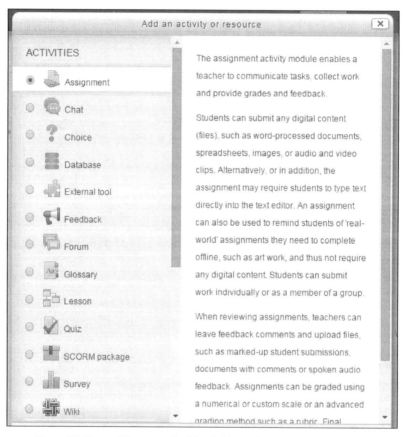

Figure 3.1: Turn editing on and add activities. Select Moodle Assignment

The assignment activity can be used to record scores for offline activities. Under **Submission types,** unselect all boxes. The learners will see a message indicating that no submission is required. Teachers can use this as a quick method to enter scores for all or some learners, which will be added up in the gradebook. Once set up, the activity can be duplicated for each week.

Try this in your test course, and then duplicate one for each week:

1. Turn editing on, and add a new activity or resource.

2. Select **Assignment,** and unselect the upload option tick boxes:

Figure 3.2: The assignment activity allows you to choose if you allow any upload methods

3. In the **Grade** box, make sure you choose **Week 2** as the grading category.

4. Use the icon next to the activity name to duplicate the activity so that you have a copy for every week.

    Set a different **Grade category** for each week each time you make a copy:

5. Drag the copies into the other weeks using the following move icon:

Teachers can organize an offline activity and use Moodle's assignment to provide written instructions. To manually enter scores for participants, select **View submissions** and enter grades. Alternatively, you can add an item to the gradebook directly as an offline task and use the quick grading feature in the Moodle gradebook to enter scores:

1. Go to your course gradebook and turn editing on.

2. Enter the marks for each person.

3. Save your grades:

Surname ▲ First name	Email address	Choose your focus artist ⇕ ✎	Painting Analysis - Say ... ⇕ ✎	Task 1 Offline activity ⇕ ✎
	Controls	⚙	⚙	⚙
Frances Banks	francesbanks231@example.com	⚙ Q	⚙ Q	⚙ 7.00
Mark Ellis	markellis267@example.com	⚙ Q	⚙ Q	⚙ 5.00
Brian Franklin	brianfrankli228@example.com	⚙ Q 10.00	⚙ Q	⚙ 10.00
Barbara Gardner	barbaragardner249@example.com	⚙ Q	⚙ Q	⚙ 4.00
Amanda Hamilton	amandahamilto205@example.com	⚙ Q	⚙ Q	⚙ 8.00
Joshua Knight	joshuaknight196@example.com	⚙ Q	⚙ Q	⚙ 0.00
Donna Taylor	donnataylor203@example.com	⚙ Q	⚙ Q	⚙ 8.00
Brenda Vasquez	brendavasquez355@example.com	⚙ Q	⚙ Q	⚙ 6.00
Gary Vasquez	garyvasquez366@example.com	⚙ Q	⚙ Q	⚙ 8.00
	Overall average	10.00		6.22

Figure 3.3: Using the Assignment activity to record offline activities

The Cup of Fate Gamification activity

You could try this suggestion (inspired by Tanya Sasse at `remixingcollegeenglish.wordpress.com`) for a weekly offline activity. Make a list of skills or values you want to encourage and assess. In digital media, we need to have a range of values and underpinning industry knowledge to ensure that our technical skills can be used in a professional environment. These include core skills such as team work, communication, ethics, and safe and sustainable work practices. These became a list of achievements that are printed as individual cards and placed in a large container. They are listed in a Moodle glossary as well with a title and a description.

At the weekly *Cup of Fate* ceremony, each learner selects a random card from the *Cup of Fate*. The class discusses what this achievement means and what you have to do to earn this achievement. As a group, they decide whether the person has done anything in the recent weeks to deserve the achievement. To earn the *Team work* badge, there are five smaller achievements that can be traded in once all of them have been collected: presenter, leader, observer, notetaker, and timekeeper.

The next time there is a team activity, people will encourage their friends to try out a new role so that they can earn an achievement in the next ceremony.

The learners are always highly engaged with this activity and take control of the conversation to explain key concepts to each other. At the end of year review, this activity receives really positive feedback. The combination of chance, ownership, interaction, and giggles covers up what is essentially a lecture on Work Health and Safety (WHS)! Instead of the teacher repetitively stating the industry expectations, the group comes to accept these as regular concepts and are more than happy to explain the rules to others (and judge) whether other people deserve to keep their achievement. This activity could be adapted for use in a webinar of an online course.

Growth mindsets and personalized learning

The Moodle **Choice** activity is a simple way to encourage a growth mindset where each learner believes in their own capacity to succeed if they consistently put in the effort. In the beginning of the course, ask the learners to indicate their perceived current skill level. After they submit their choice, they will see what other people have selected (if you enable this feature). They will probably be encouraged to find that other people have selected similar skill levels. Towards the end of the course, invite the learners to do this choice activity again and indicate whether they have gone up a level or two. Instead of setting a *finish line* with a deadline for all learners, you can set up personalized learning by asking the learners to self-assess their current level, set a new goal, and reflect on the progress they have made. This will take you just ten minutes to implement with Moodle's simplest tool!

Another suggestion is to use the Choice activity as a quick feedback activity on the effectiveness of a teaching session and a way to quickly identify those who would like some assistance. Try adding this feedback activity to your test course:

1. Add an activity.
2. Select Choice.

3. Add a few choices (you can add content in the description or embed a video):

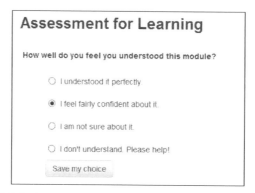

Figure 3.4: Polling your learners is easy with the Choice activity in Moodle

Creating teachable moments through suspense and hope

A highly effective method of teaching is to stop intermittently during a lecture and take a poll. Why invest in special clicker technology to achieve this when the Moodle **Choice** activity can be set up as a simple poll? Here is an example of how this can be used in a face-to-face setting. Try this in your test course:

1. Set up three quick polls in Moodle relating to your topic. Each one will have a different web address, something like this: `http://school.demo.moodle.net/mod/choice/view.php?id=170`

2. At three intervals during your lecture, ask the learners to form small groups and discuss the answers for 5 minutes.

3. Shorten the links into something like `bit.ly/2015zwq` so that you can write these on a whiteboard (go to `www.bit.ly` or `www.goo.gl` to shorten the URL).

4. Using a *bring your own device* approach, ask one person from each group to submit their group answer to the poll.

5. You can configure the **Choice** activity to automatically show what other people have answered, but in this case, you will want to turn this option off to build the suspense and create a teachable moment. Imagine you are about to announce the winner of this year's X Factor. You are holding that piece of paper in your hand, and everyone is totally focused on what you will say next. You have a small window of opportunity here to deliver content knowing that learners are all eyes and ears. They have committed to an answer, therefore, they are invested in knowing the response. When the interest wanes, you can reveal the answer and move on:

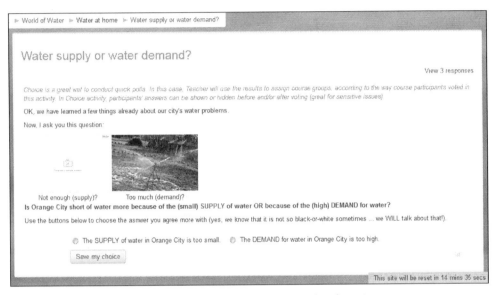

Figure 3.5: The Choice activity can be used in a lot of creative ways

You really have to try this yourself to see how a room of sleepy learners can be transformed into attentive listeners through the introduction of risk and hope (uncertain rewards). Do some research on the *Neuroscience of Learning* by the University of Bristol that explains what is happening here:

"Our motivation to engage with a task is coded in the brain by an uptake of dopamine in the mid-brain. This signal is enhanced when rewards are uncertain.

The diagram shows the dopaminergic response (the amount of dopamine generated in the brain) from different visual stimuli that vary in how reliably they predict a reward. These three stimuli signal that a reward will arrive with a probability 'P' of 0%, 50% and 100%.

A) When a stimulus signals 100% certainty of a reward arriving, a spike of dopamine is generated when the stimulus is observed but nothing occurs when the reward is received (because it is totally predictable).

B) In contrast, a stimulus that has never been associated with reward generates no dopamine, but a spike occurs when a totally unexpected reward arrives.

C) When a stimulus associated with 50% likely reward is seen, it generates a spike and then the dopamine ramps up until the outcome is revealed. Averaged over time, the uncertain reward thus generates a greater dopaminergic response than either certain or totally unexpected reward ... Measurements suggest the brain's reward response peaks when rewards are 50% ."

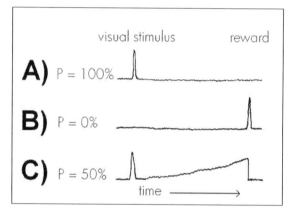

Figure 3.6: Our motivation to engage with a task is coded in the brain by an uptake of dopamine in the mid-brain

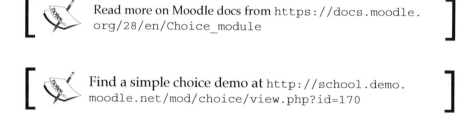

Read more on Moodle docs from https://docs.moodle.org/28/en/Choice_module

Find a simple choice demo at http://school.demo.moodle.net/mod/choice/view.php?id=170

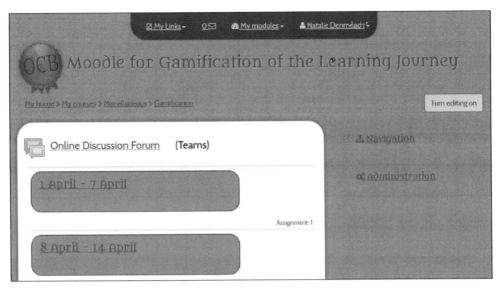

Figure 3.7: Your test course should now have 4 weeks with a few offline assignments, a forum, and some choices

Summary

The Moodle assignment can be configured in many different ways to implement Gamification. This takes some creative thinking to imagine what else these basic activities can achieve. It may be tempting to purchase a premade Gamification platform, however, when the simplest of all activities, the **Choice** activity, is used with a strong pedagogical support, this can be highly effective in raising motivation. Take some time to set this up once, and then duplicate the activity for reuse. Moodle allows you to import an activity from one course to another saving you from repeating your efforts.

Moodle's simple activities, such as assignment and choice, retain the power to create in the hands of the expert. At any point, you can easily update your activities. While other eLearning content produced by a team of specialists may look highly professional, it can quickly become outdated and too hard to change. Sometimes, this needs to go through a series of authorization or format changes to be republished. Ownership of the content becomes unclear, and funding is often not set aside for the lifetime maintenance of the product. The time pressure to meet learning outcomes may not match the time available to use the eLearning package. These are the underlying reason why many teachers avoid using premade content packages. Giving teachers the option to start with a blank Moodle course and the freedom to be creative can result in something that is more engaging for learners, even though it may not look as slick as a high-end package.

In the next chapter, you will see that advances in technology are empowering teachers to design course layouts that are easier for learners to navigate. Game designers use minimal layouts with brief text to introduce content gradually. We will discuss how the Moodle feature of conditional activities enables you to reveal the content of your course based on learner interactions.

Plugin: PoodLL

This repository allows you to record audio or video directly into your Moodle HTML areas. It also allows students to draw pictures or take webcam "snaps." The widget repository allow students to add "PoodLL widgets" such as stopwatches and flashcards to Moodle activities.

4
Passing the Gateway (Conditional Activities)

This chapter is about restricting activities until prerequisites have been met. Moodle offers a wide range of easily configurable gateways to check and ensure progress before new content or activities are released. These checks may be based on self-assessment, peer-assessment, computer-based marking, or teacher grading.

Allow 60 minutes to set up conditional activities and restrictions. (Be warned that this could take hours or days if you get hooked to the new powers you have acquired in Moodle!)

The chapter will cover the following topics:

- Minimalistic design
- Conditional activities
- Auto-completion
- Restriction options

Minimalistic course layout design

The web is quickly moving towards simple, clean, and minimalist layouts with large fonts, plenty of white spaces, and single column flexible designs. The use of different devices and screen sizes with touch input is driving this change. One of the biggest criticisms of Moodle courses is navigation. Imagine if your learners walked through the door on the first day, and you handed them every exam, reference, and textbook required for the entire course in one go! Yet, this is what we often try to do in one Moodle course. This topic will give suggestions on the alternate ways of designing your Moodle courses to create a better **User Experience design** (**UX design**) and an effective **User Interface** (**UI**).

"Most Learning Management Systems let learners and teachers perform learning tasks. We need to move these systems along the spectrum so they can provide experiences instead."

– Joyce Seitzinger, 2015

The Impressionists demonstration course shows how content can be revealed based on actions. This is not hard but it can be time consuming. The course is best experienced as a learner. Log in to the demo course with the `student` login username and the `moodle` password.

You can do this through the administration block, **Switch role to ...student**. In some cases, this will be good enough to meet your testing purposes. However, when you are testing out Gamification, your gradebook will not function correctly unless you are enrolled as a student and fully participate. It is strongly suggested that you make a test student account and have two browsers open. It is strongly suggested that you make a test student account and have two browsers open. (Yes, I repeated this because I really wanted to get your attention and save you the hours of frustration I experienced.) In Chrome, you can log in as the teacher in editing mode. In Firefox, you can log in as a student and refresh your screen to check how the changes look. Web developers always test their content in multiple browsers to identify any problems. As most of your learners now have smart phones or tablets, you should check how your Moodle course looks in a smaller layout. In Firefox, use the middle button in the top-right corner of your browser to make the window flexible. Now, make this half the size of your screen and look at a few web pages. Some pages will shrink to the scale of the current window size, some pages will cut off important content, and others will reshuffle and/or hide unnecessary content. How does your course look to a student using a tablet device, the size of which is half of an average desktop's monitor size (about 1000 pixels)?

Figure 4.1: This window shows content in a small layout. Responsive Bootstrap 3+-based themes are recommended for a Moodle site

In the preceding figure, you can see that the grid of six photos (almost) fits nicely on a smaller screen. The navigation block has been moved to the bottom of the layout. This is called "Responsive Web Design". Moodle themes based on Bootstrap 3, such as the Shoehorn theme by Gareth Barnard, are recommended because of their flexibility to work on both large desktop screen layouts and small mobile screen layouts. You don't have to know much about web design to make your Moodle courses mobile friendly. The trick is to keep it simple as mobile-friendly designs are elegantly minimal. Focus on what you want the learner to do now and try to remove everything else from the screen layout. As few words as possible, and clear choices, work best for mobile functionality and on larger desktop monitors as well.

Mobile friendly design:

- Avoid the use of the "click" word—use "select" instead.

- Don't use Flash (`.swf`) content, as it won't work on tablets or phones (right-click to see if the web content is developed using Flash).

- If you don't have Moodle 2.8 +, which allows autosizing of images in Bootstrap-based themes, you can apply a class called `img-responsive` in the image attributes options:

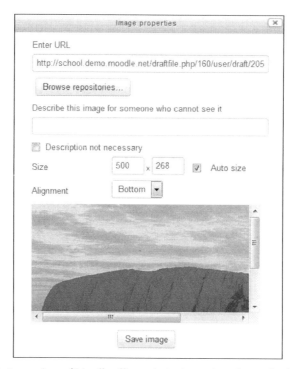

Figure 4.2: Later versions of Moodle offer an Auto size option when uploading an image

Revealing content

The student can see a limited amount of content in the Impressionists course. The entire second section of the course will be revealed once certain conditions have been met. In this demo course, the learner cannot proceed until they have chosen a focus artist. Since the implementation of this feature, Moodle course creators can apply logic in the same way that game programmers map out a series of linked activities with and/or pre-requisites.

In a classroom setting, this feature can also be used to save on repetitive administration tasks such as collecting acknowledgements of important document distribution. Instead of you chasing the students, they will be wondering why they can't access what their friends can see and they will have to go back to catch up on the links that they have missed. The Moodle LMS is designed to free up your time by automating these types of reporting and admin activities of teachers. Learners spend a lot of their time in school waiting, which leads to boredom. When you don't have to manually walk around collecting signatures on paper, the entire school day becomes more productive. After everybody has viewed the document, the Moodle reporting activities will show the names of the people who have completed the activity, which you can download in Excel format and print permanent offline records. A 30-minute task just became a 3-minute task.

Completion tracking

You already may have **Activity completion** in the settings of any Moodle activity. If not, the Moodle administrator can enable course completion for the site:

1. Navigate to **Administration | Site administration | Advanced features**:

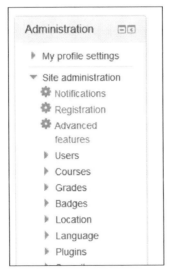

Figure 4:3: Moodle admins can enable advanced features for your Moodle site

2. Tick the **Enable completion tracking** checkbox and **Enable conditional access**:

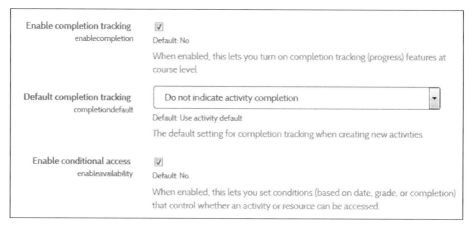

Figure 4.4: Change the Moodle site settings to track completion

3. A teacher can then enable or disable course completion for their course by setting **Enable completion tracking** to **Yes** in **Administration | Course administration | Edit settings**. (This enables the use of **Activity completion** too.)

4. Course creators can choose to enable completion tracking:

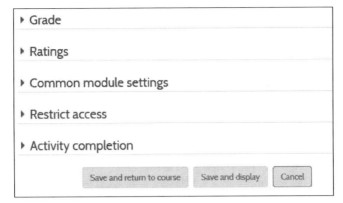

Figure 4.5: If you don't see the last **Activity completion** section in an activity, then completion tracking must first be enabled in the Moodle course, or site, settings.

Completion requirements

In *Chapter 2, Communication and Collaboration (Labels and Forums)* we added a forum. If you have used the free MoodleCloud site or your own test site, you can continue to follow along. Let's take this a step further and use completion criteria to act as a gateway. In the forum settings, select **Activity completion**. Choose the following:

- **Learners must receive a grade to complete this activity**. (This means that learners must have their avatar rated by at least one person.)
- **Learners must post at least one reply**. (This means that if you post a request for people to reply with a `Hello Message`, they must reply.)

Each student will have to reply (answer) to your question (post) before they can see other's replies. You can use the reports in Moodle to quickly see who is on task and use this as a gateway to prevent further progress through the course until the completion criteria has been met:

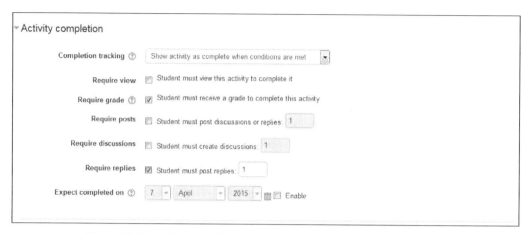

Figure 4.6: Set up the criteria for what "completion" is required for this activity

1. Select an entire section by selecting **Edit Summary** at the head of the section (**Week 2**) in Moodle and go to the **Restrict access** options.

2. Select the **Add restrictions** button and choose **Activity completion**. In the drop-down box, select the forum you have made as the activity.

3. Select the eye icon to completely hide the section. (By default, the restricted section is grayed out and a brief message is displayed to the learner.)

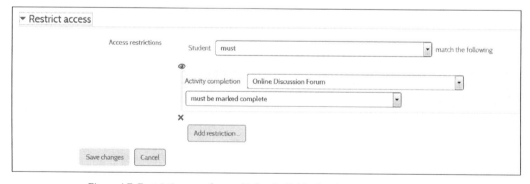

Figure 4.7: Restrictions can be applied to individual activities or entire sections

4. Repeat this for **Week 3** and **Week 4**. As soon as the learner completes the forum activity in the way you have specified, they will see the content for weeks 2, 3, and 4. If you have more weeks, you can restrict access to weeks 5, 6, and 7 based on conditions in an activity in **Week 4**. You are making a daisy chain of activities that require passing through a series of gates. How cool is that! Do you feel like a game designer yet? The course is now being progressively revealed:

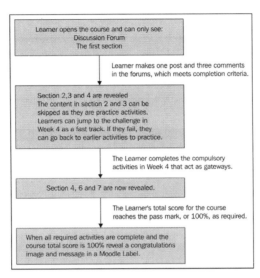

Figure 4.8: Plan a series of activities which are either optional or compulsory gateways

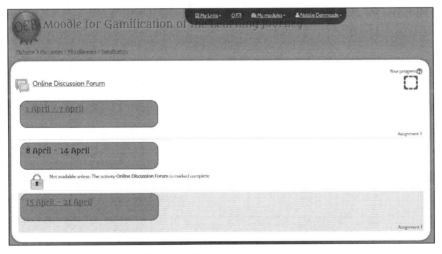

Figure 4.9: Entire sections are hidden and revealed to keep a minimal layout

5. Weeks 3 and 4 only become visible once the forum is marked as complete:

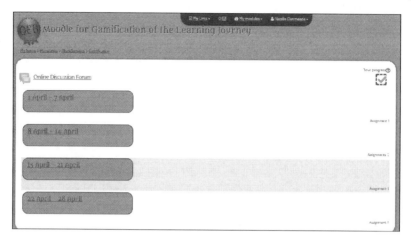

Figure 4.10: Once Forum Activity is complete, more content becomes available

Completion options

You can imagine how this plays out like an interactive game depending on what the learner has (or hasn't) completed. Each activity in Moodle has different completion options available. Even the simple *Label* can be set to be marked as *completed manually* by the learner. This can act as an on/off switch for your game logic:

1. Add an activity or a resource and choose **Label**.
2. In **Activity completion,** choose **Students can manually mark the activity as completed**.

Create some additional activities that are advanced or slightly off topic, and restrict their access to be shown only if the on/off switch you created is ticked by the learner. This is the essence of personalized learning! Here are a few other on/off switches you could try out in your own test course:

*   **Would you like to show hints for this section?** (Ticking the box reveals a whole lot of other labels with instructions throughout your course and can quite possibly double the length of your course but only for those people who prefer it this way.)

*   **Finding this too easy?** Tick the box to switch to Hard Mode. (This would turn off introductory levels and let the learners jump straight to a final assessment.)

- **Did you find this topic useful?** (Tick to indicate yes—check your reports to see the response.)
- **Have you read xyz and are you ready to do your assessment?** (Tick required to proceed.)

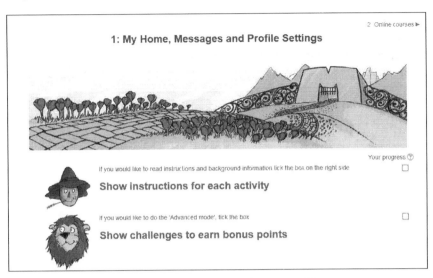

Figure 4.11: Use labels as on/off switches to reveal the content

If you create a label with **Tick the box if you want to do extra work**, the learner will probably not feel motivated. Changing the wording slightly has a powerful effect: **Tick the box to show extra activities to earn bonus points**. The gaming world has given us a whole new language that we can use to communicate with gamers. Simply switching to their dialect has amazing effects.

Teachers will never really be cool because we will get it wrong, but I find that teenagers are generous and really appreciate the effort. I usually involve them in the design, which helps with ownership and reduces complaints.

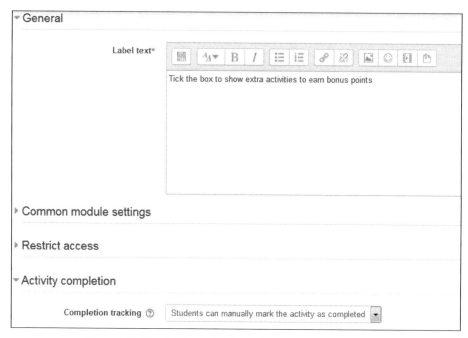

Figure 4.12: Simple Moodle labels can be used as on/off switches

The *Follow the Orange Brick Road* course is a demonstration of a Moodle course using conditional activities, labels as on/off switches, and other game elements. You can unlock each letter of the M-O-O-D-L-E word by completing the challenges presented.

Learners are offered three different paths through this journey to reach Emerald City. By default, the course can be completed in a fast-tracked mode with little reading to allow the learners to explore the environment on their own terms. If they prefer to be guided, they can watch videos and read more information on what is required to complete the activities. Opportunities for social interactivity are put in place through glossary and forum comments and ratings, and by encouraging the use of Moodle blogs and tags. The learners are given opportunities for active participation via multiple channels and feedback from teachers, peers, Moodle tools, and self-assessment.

The narrative used in this course establishes that the learner needs to master basic Moodle skills while going on a journey down the Orange Brick road to enter Emerald City. Progress reports through this journey are given using graphics in the summary of each topic that shows progress and a custom progress bar with golden stars (replacing ticks and crosses). A scoreboard has been implemented using the Configurable Reports plugin. The current course total and time spent on the course is displayed as **heads up display (HUD)**. Giving frequent feedback on the progress can be very motivating.

There are three levels available to the learners: basic, advanced, and course creator. The course creator level is based on participants self-selecting to join a group that provides access to hidden content. A badge is awarded at each level. If the participants select the bonus level points, they will receive the special Gold badge.

Figure 4.13: Enroll in the free "Orange Brick Road" demo course

View the *Orange Brick Road* course with Gamification features. Anyone is welcome to register and enroll at `http://demo.klevar.com/course/view.php?id=2`.

Labels with restrictions used as adaptive messaging

The designer of the very successful game, *Plants vs. Zombies* used adaptive messaging to provide hints at the right time and not undermine the joy of discovery. How can you do this in Moodle? Activities such as the lesson and quiz allow us to provide feedback for errors but are time-consuming to set up. You can do this much easier, and quicker, with labels, which can be formatted nicely with images or icons. Set up a few different hints as you would if you were walking around the classroom adapting your response to each person. Use the restriction settings to show the label depending on the grade they have achieved in a quiz or other activity. You can use "Learner MUST match the following" or "MUST NOT" to ensure that the hint is only displayed if the score is within a certain range. Once they have made the choice, the label will not be displayed:

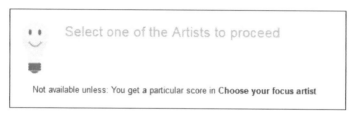

Figure 4.13: Set this hint to disappear once the person has made a choice

Moodle labels to create minimalistic design layouts

Moodle labels with restrictions are a good way to get past the dilemma of a welcome tutorial message and a cluttered screen. You can use a label that is restricted as soon as the learner has received more than one percent of the course total. The message will now be hidden after receiving any grade. When they have achieved 100 percent, a label will appear saying **Congratulations**. This approach keeps the current content in focus. Avoid having the initial one-third of your layout taken up with introductory information (or taking up a third of your page with a giant corporate banner and logo) which people have to constantly scroll past to start working. The learner needs to see what they have to do next with minimal amount of clutter. This is especially true for content on smaller mobile screens.

View your course on a mobile device to see what content should be removed or repositioned. How many user options (links) are on this page? The more the learners have to read to make an action decision, the less willpower they will have. We can learn how dangerous clutter is from a Stanford University experiment on the use of our limited pool of cognitive resources at `http://seriouspony.com/blog/2013/7/24/your-app-makes-me-fat`:

> *What you consume here, you take from there. Not just their attention, not just their time, but their ability to be the person they are when they are at their best. When they have ample cognitive resources. When they can think, solve-problems, and exercise self-control. When they can create, make connections, and stay focused.*

Take a hardcopy of your Moodle page and highlight anything that is duplicated. Have you provided multiple navigation options back to the home page? Is this link really necessary—now? A cluttered page layout is like presenting a series of roundabouts with 20 options. If the Moodle home page has these links, then having them appear on your course pages will only lead to cluttering. Be savage. Google won the fight to be the best search engine because they only used a simple layout. Our current eLearning LMS culture is quickly moving away from multicolumn cluttered layouts. Simple and elegant with a lot of white space is the new cool trend in web design.

Game layouts do not position their company banner or logo on every screen or fill the footer with links to dozens of other possible choices that the player may want to make in the future. Keep your LMS layout minimal. You should keep introductory material off your main screen layout:

Figure 4.14: Google Search 1998 (10 links to user options): The minimalist design has become their trademark. It was eventually trimmed down even more than this!

Figure 4.15: Yahoo Search 1997 (50 links to user options): LMS designs are rapidly moving away
from dozens of links and multiple column layouts

Summary

Since the implementation of conditional activities, Moodle has shifted to a whole
new level as a versatile Gamification platform. Through simple labels and restriction
settings, you are now more like a game designer. Games will look better than Moodle
courses because they have professional graphic design teams (and a massive budget),
but at least you have the power to limit how much information and how many choices
are available on one screen layout. First, you set the completion criteria for an activity,
and then you use restrict access rules on new activities that you design.

Use your powers wisely. Plan out a sequence of activities and thoughtfully place
gates to control flow and access. Sticky notes are a great way to visualize these
pathways. Use these conditional activities to minimize your layout. Only show the
minimum amount of information to get to the next step. Remember to use a second
student account to make sure you have configured the course correctly.

Choosing a mobile-friendly Moodle theme is important. Gareth Barnard's Bootstrap (Mobile First) templates are highly recommended. These are recommended not just for technical reasons but also because choosing a plugin is similar to committing to a relationship with the developer. Developers of plugins for Moodle may create a great piece of code that they wish to share as a one-off event but have no funding in place to check the code every six months as the core Moodle code is upgraded. Especially when choosing a course theme or format, you need to choose a developer who has a consistent record of contributions and is committed (funded) to updating their plugin to keep up with Moodle Core updates. These developers are often paid to do a small piece of work and generously share it back with the open-source community. It is worth searching on Moodle.org and making a list of these highly committed Moodle plugin developers and ensuring that they stay with the community through small donations or referrals for paid work.

 Read more about conditional activities on Moodle Docs: `https://docs.moodle.org/28/en/Conditional_activities`

The next chapter will explore how games reframe failure and create resilience through rapid and frequent feedback. You can start to create your own leveling up systems that make learning goals more appealing and achievable.

Plugin: Collapsible Topics

Each topic can be collapsed and multiple columns can be set up, which can be used for topic- or week- or day-based formats. All sections except zero have a toggle that display that particular section. One or more sections can be displayed at any given time. Toggles are persistent on a per browser session per course basis but can be made to persist longer by a small code change.

5
Feedback on Progress (Marking Guides and Scales)

This chapter is about setting up Moodle assignments and providing effective feedback through the use of a comment bank.

Allow 30 minutes to set up an assignment with a marking guide.

This chapter will cover the following topics:

- Assignment submission
- Grading options
- Feedback

Assessing progress

So far, the course design has not used any formal online assessment. We have encouraged peer interaction and peer-assessment of the avatar in a forum. We set up self-assessment through a choice activity. We set up a Moodle assignment with nothing to upload, which the teacher can use to enter scores for participation in offline activities.

The reasoning behind the design was to welcome people to this new course through an onboarding process. We have provided opportunities to build connections with other people in the course and build up their feeling of competence. They could use activities in a low-risk setting to build their confidence in using Moodle. In your course, you would do more of this, but this simplified demonstration shows that people are more likely to use Moodle activities if you set up a low-risk non-assessable mini version as a tutorial. If people can imagine an event, it reduces the anxiety and they are more likely to take a risk.

With this foundation in place, it is time to provide some assessable challenges using the Moodle assignment and marking guides.

Marking guides

You can communicate the rules of the challenge using a marking guide. Create a new assignment (**Add an activity...**). Then edit the assignment. When you view this activity in Moodle, do the following:

1. In the **ADMINISTRATION** block, select **Advanced grading**. In the drop-down box, choose **Marking guide** or **Grading guide** (US):

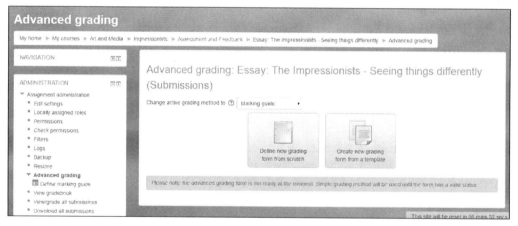

Figure 5.1: Under ADMINISTRATION | Assignment administration, choose "Advanced grading" to define a marking guide

2. While viewing an assignment, select **Advanced grading** in the **ADMINISTRATION** block.

3. Define a new grading form from scratch, and enter your criterion and maximum marks. This is an example of a quick way to set up gaming levels:

    ° Criterion 1 name: The **Bronze** level–type the names of five plants (50 points)

    ° Criterion 2 name: The **Silver** level–research which plant families these belong to (35 points)

    ° Criterion 3 name: The **Gold** level–split your list to identify which of these plants would be called "weeds" or non-noxious plants (15 points)

4. You can use the **Frequently used comments** bank to store encouraging playful phrases such as:

    ° "You are almost there ... try again. You can resubmit your work up to five times to improve your score. Only your highest mark will be recorded."

    ° "That was a Gold Level answer—congratulations!"

5. Make sure that you tick the box to show the **Marking guide** to the learners.

Observe the types of feedback offered in video games and use this as an inspiration for what you could add to your feedback comment bank. It is worth spending some time to add these comments because your marking guides can be saved and reused as a starting point for another assignment.

For some practice, try adding a few feedback comments to this example marking guide on the Mount Orange School demo course: `htp://school.demo.moodle.net/ grade/grading/manage.php?areaid=30`

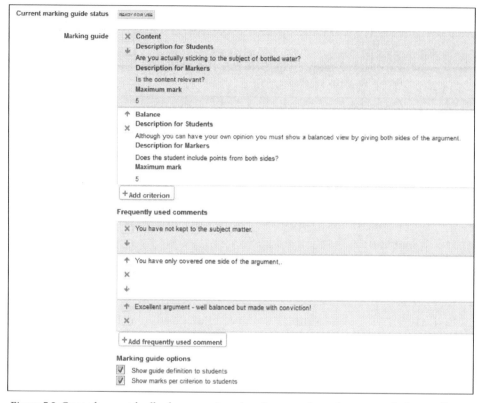

Figure 5.2: Create frequent feedback comments and easily re-use throughout your whole Moodle site

Delayed feedback feeds anxiety

Once an assignment has been submitted, the learner must wait for the teacher to mark the work and provide feedback. This delay is a source of anxiety for most people, especially high achievers, according to Carol Dweck. In games, the feedback is instant and far more frequent than in education. The feedback usually provides you a chance to repeatedly try to increase your score. Think of quick feedback as a major way to reduce anxiety.

The assignment is a very popular way of submitting work in Moodle, but how can we use other Moodle activities to provide quicker and more frequent feedback?

- Use peer ratings in forum posts (as in **Week 1**).

- The choice module immediately shows a learner what other people in the class are doing or thinking.

- The Moodle wiki allows each person to rate others.

- The feedback module is an easy way to set up an interactive pathway based on answers. If learners answer a question incorrectly, they are directed to some background material. You can set up a link to another activity once they have been through the feedback process.

- The quiz uses instant computer-based marking. You can display the quiz results block to show a leader board for each group.

A series of Moodle lessons are a very powerful method to provide rapid automated feedback. You can set up prerequisites, time limits, number of re-tries, and hints. Based on their results, you can display the next lesson (easy or hard) to match their ability.

The problem for most teachers is the time required for preparation. It would take time to learn how to use these Moodle activities to provide faster feedback to learners. (However, it takes time to mark all the submitted paper assessments by hand as well!). This book has been purposely started with tips on the easiest and most effective Moodle activities: the forum, choice, and assignment. Once you have mastered these, then make a commitment to explore an additional activity each semester or year. Eventually, you will have the entire range at your disposal, but you really don't have to read up on everything before you get started.

Decide which feedback activities are the best for your learners at the different phases of the learning journey:

- **Phase 1 (onboarding)**: You want to send a clear message that their opinions, ideas, and questions are welcome. This feedback should come from both peers and the teacher. At this point, set it up so they can't fail as the options are very narrow.

- **Phase 2 (problem solving)**: The learner is presented with a series of challenges at the level that are appropriate for their current ability in this context. The feedback used here is about identifying skills gaps and strengths. Self-assessment is very useful at this early stage. Peer-assessment is less intimidating than teacher assessment and can do a lot to build up confidence as well as encourage collaborative learning.

- **Phase 3 (master)**: This is the stage where the learner needs more formal feedback on the performance through a series of incremental challenges to build-up confidence.

- **Phase 4 (expert)**: The learner is really past the point of relying on feedback now.

- **Phase 5 (visionary)**: The learner starts telling you how the learning activities could be better. Have you set up channels to receive that feedback?

If your school has tight guidelines on how you assess and provide feedback, consider setting up a Moodle course and badges that do not replace this system. Use the Moodle course as a communication channel, collaboration space, and for practice activities. Keep formal assessments out of your Gamification design.

Read more about marking guides on Moodle docs available at: `https://docs.moodle.org/28/en/Marking_guide`

Video tutorial: `http://vivaelearning.com/-Moodle-Marking-Guide-Moodle-Tutorial/`

Leveling up with scales or letters

There is a world of difference between being told that you are at the **Bronze** level and receiving an F grade. In reality, they are the same but the language used creates a different mental concept. Professor Dweck describes this as encouraging a fixed mindset or a growth mindset, (see: `http://mindsetonline.com/`). Her research shows that rewarding effort and process rather than ability builds resilience in learners. Learners begin to understand their brain as "plastic" and believe that they can grow and learn constantly. This challenges the concept of having a set IQ and the idea that people are simply "dumb" or "smart".

School reports often use terms such as "Pass" or "Fail". This is possible to replicate by using a custom scale in Moodle to display a percentage as a word. If there are two items in your custom scale, then a result of anything less than 50 percent will have the **FAIL** word displayed or above 50 percent will display the **PASS** word.

Why not try a few other variations to make this feel more like a game and encourage resilience:

Incomplete, Complete (50% each)

Observer, Problem Solver, Master, Mentor, Guru (equal scale of 20% each)

Junior Designer, Senior Designer, Director, Executive Producer (equal scale of 25% each)

It is possible to use unequal divisions within a Moodle gradebook by customizing the traditional letters such as A, B,C, D, E, and F with your own phrases and choosing the lowest/highest score for each bracket:

Edit grade letters		
Highest	Lowest	Letter
100.00 %	30.00 %	Master.
29.99 %	10.00 %	Problem solver.
9.99 %	0.00 %	Observer.

Figure 5.3: Scales use equal divisions, whereas letters can be assigned unequal ranges

Summary

This chapter explained the activities in Moodle that provide feedback. You were encouraged to think about the different types of feedback that are required throughout a learning journey. You can save yourself some time by using the marking guide feedback comment bank. Other teachers can share your comments across your Moodle site by reusing your template. Why not get a few Moodlers together and set up some templates?

[Read more on Moodle docs at `https://docs.moodle.org/28/en/ Grades_FAQ`]

In the next chapter, you will be transported to the future of digital credentialing through badges. As we move towards a global community, organizations and individuals will want to transport the evidence of skills from one context to another. Although our current assessment systems are based on principles of validity, authenticity, fairness, and sufficient evidence, we are still struggling to manage the ongoing problems of cheating, deception, corruption, and ambiguity in assessment criteria. Moving away from a paper-based system offers some solutions by cross-referencing the claims of achievement with the online portfolios of work and using the readily available details of the evidence and criteria attached to a credential. Badges do not have to replace traditional qualifications, certificates, grades, and transcripts. In some ways, they are the evolution of personal resumes and in other ways, they are really something quite unique.

Plugin: My Grades

The My Grades block provides a display of all enrolled courses, overall grades and links to grade reports from the My Home page. If you use "Scales" as your Course Total these will display on the My Home Page to indicate progress in the course so far. (You don't need this block if you have the latest Moodle 2.9 version with the new Grades page).

6
Mastery Achieved (Badges and Motivation)

This chapter is about using Moodle LMS to easily issue Open Badges to recognize achievements. The **Open Badge Infrastructure (OBI)** is the underlying technology that supports badge issuing, collection, and display. Each learner creates their own online backpack to keep and display digital badges. You can think of this as the next generation of digital resumes, but this is far more than just that.

Allow 10 minutes to set the activity completion criteria and add a new badge in Moodle.

The chapter will cover the following topics:

- Badge creation
- Criteria, exporting, and displaying
- Peer badging
- Player motivation and individual needs

Creating badges

Open Badges make more sense when you see them in action, so let's get started and afterwards we can explain what we have achieved. Decide on two badges you would like to design for your test course. Perhaps a Welcome badge and another badge to represent an achievement. Moodle will accept any square image as a badge. The image will be resized to 90x90 pixels, so one or two words is the most you can fit on a small badge. Here are a few tips to find images for badges:

- Search for "Free icon packs" on Google. Games and websites use these packs of images, and they make great badges. Try this website: `http://www.freepik.com/`

- Make your own badges at sites such as this one: `https://www.openbadges.me/`

- Use Photoshop brushes or stamps to make badges: `http://wegraphics.net/downloads/vintage-badge-templates-brushes-vectors-and-textures/`

Figure 6.1: Badges must be square and will be resized to 90 x 90 pixels in Moodle. Make sure your badges are legible even if they are small

Badge criteria

Try uploading an image to create a Digital Open Badge for your test course:

1. In the **Administration** block, navigate to **Badges | Add a new badge**.

2. Type in a name and description that will be displayed with the image you upload, that is, `Welcome` and `Test Badge`.

3. Enter your name and contact e-mail as the issuer, which will be permanently linked to the badge.

4. For this test set the badge to be automatically awarded if someone meets the forum completion activity that we added in **Week 1**. (You can choose to "manually issue" the badge or set "automatic issue" based on the criteria defined in **Activity completion**.).

5. Add some of your own text to the **Welcome** message (this may be a secret clue to be used later).

6. Select **Enable access** when the badge is ready to be used.

7. Save the changes and that is it! Moodle does the rest of the work for you by embedding all the criteria and issuer metadata into the image to create a Digital Open Badge.

Figure 6.2: Setting up a badge in Moodle takes 2 minutes

Throughout a learner's life, they will be members of many educational institutions. Mozilla Firefox has set up an independent online place for people to save and share their verified Open Badges. Sign up for an account to start your own "Digital Backpack": https://backpack.openbadges.org/backpack/login.

Each person can choose whether to send badges earned in Moodle to their Digital Backpack. Also, they can group their badges into private and public collections to share through social media or another LMS:

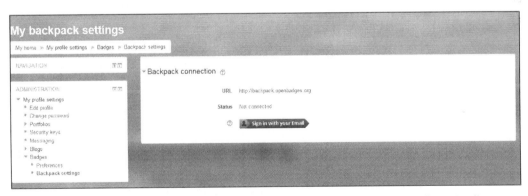

Figure 6.3: In your profile settings, you can choose to connect an external "Backpack" to Moodle

Traditional resume	Next generation digital badges
The learner receives a periodical report on educational achievements.	The learner completes an online activity and receives one or more digital badges.
The learner completes a qualification and receives a transcript and a verified certificate.	The learner receives a digital badge with details of the criteria required to earn this badge. Badges are grouped into collections.
The learner creates a paper resume and compiles qualifications from different places over their lifetime.	The learner exports their digital badges from a variety of places into a central backpack that is not owned or managed by an institution. They make a collection of badges public or private.
A potential employer reads the resume and may contact referees or compare a portfolio of work to the statements of educational achievements.	A potential employer sees the Digital Badge Backpack and can follow links to the issuer's name and web address for more details. They may contact referees or compare a portfolio of work to the statements of educational achievements.
The paper resume is unverified. Certificates can be easily copied and digitally altered. The credibility of the issuer may be unknown.	The hidden metadata attached to the digital badge cannot simply be photoshopped onto any image. The links provided go directly to an issuing identity's website, which is difficult to fake. The credibility of the issuer may be unknown.

Acceptance of digital badges

Leading universities, such as Deakin in Australia, have implanted this next generation accreditation system alongside traditional structures. Both systems can be used in a complementary fashion. See `http://www.deakindigital.com` and `http://www.afr.com/news/policy/education/digital-badge-sets-students-on-new-course-20140216-ixrxr`.

The question arises about what a badge represents. Similar to currency, language, and any symbol, meaning and value are dynamic and operate at both local and global scales. We don't need to develop an international curriculum and agree on the levels of credentials before we start using digital badges. This process will likely unfold over time through the work of the Badge Alliance, W3C, Clinton Global Initiative fund, and IMS Initiatives. (See `http://erinknight.com/post/116992067678/ims-digital-credentialing-initiative`) In the meantime, much like the debate over the fluctuating value of currency, locally-defined badges with meaning in a small context are as important as the global-level interchange.

For example, Coursera's MOOC on Gamification commenced with a large majestic creature flying into a virtual world. Professor Werbach later explained that this creature symbolized his very high level of achievement in "World of Warcraft". Although the depth of meaning and symbolism went over most people's heads, this doesn't mean that the symbol is of no value. It meant a lot to the people who were meant to understand this. Your collection of digital badges, like other symbols and iconography, will have a meaning within the circles you wish to participate.

Peer-assessed badges

Badges are not just digital resumes for potential employers as a micro-credentialing system. By delegating assessment to learners through peer-assessed badges, you tap into a core human need to belong. Status within the class is a very strong motivator. The challenge is to set up a range of badges that are to be earned to appeal to different player types and recognize different skills.

In Moodle, there are roles with varying levels of access, for example, teacher, non-editing teacher, student, and so on. Usually, it is only the teacher who can issue badges, but you can set up a custom role and enable that role to issue badges. Alternatively, you can set up a new Moodle course with very little content and assign the role of non-editing teachers to the students of the class. They will be able to issue badges and not edit or change any other content.

A formal graduation often happens months after a qualification has been completed and involves a whole campus. Why not consider a class graduation ceremony towards the end of the year where you create a celebration ritual. Peers could award badges in person, and you could later issue the digital badge manually in Moodle.

Will badges motivate everybody?

If you decide to use feedback systems of points badges and leaderboards, you will first need to develop empathy for what motivates and demotivates other people. Receiving a badge may not hold any appeal to you or the idea might even annoy you as seemingly childish, but would it stop you from learning? When you design an activity loop, the motivation and feedback that you put into place will not have the same effect on all the learners. Having no effect is acceptable. Being aware of the people on whom this has a detrimental effect is important.

 Try setting up a group of badges, so people can choose which ones they want to achieve. Reward a range of behaviors, effort, and process as well as mastery.

The first time you try out an idea, try a low-tech or offline practice run, and then reflect on how you can modify the process to better suit you and your learners. One of the main decisions that you need to make is between an egalitarian approach where anyone can work through the levels to become a Guru, or a competitive model where there can be only one top position. Why not ask your class to collaboratively decide on the criteria to earn peer-awarded badges? This is an effective exercise in reflection.

Read more on Moodle Docs: `https://docs.` `moodle.org/28/en/Badges`

Personally, I thought I was indifferent to badge points and other tangible rewards until I received a badge on Moodle.org for being a "Particularly helpful Moodler". It really brought a smile to my face, and I know that when I post in forums, I will get a little icon that shows everybody my achievement. In this context, the badge is a way for the Moodle community to thank me for the efforts that I have put in. I appreciate that.

Summary

This chapter has introduced you to the use of badges as symbols of achievement to motivate and provide feedback to learners. Leading institutions are finding that Open Badges can be a highly effective way to increase motivation. Kaplan University shared results of their study.

See `http://campustechnology.com/` `articles/2013/06/27/kaplan-study-gamification-and-` `badging-succeed-in-the-online-classroom.aspx`

The "badging" aspect of gamification, using visual representations to stand for an achievement or accomplishment, yielded increased student engagement of up to 17 percent in time actively engaged over non-badged counterparts, according to program findings. Also, when harder tasks were added to the courses, 60 percent of students elected to complete the more difficult assignment to earn the related badge. Grades increased as well in gamified courses, with up to a 9 percent increase in student marks. Increases were also seen across the board in class attendance and discussion board posts for students in gamified courses.

Personally, you may not be motivated by a need to obtain a black belt in karate, an Order of Australia Medal, OBE, a Victoria Cross, a sporting trophy, or a Gold Logie, yet other people are highly motivated by these symbols of achievement. The way you design, distribute, and celebrate badges in your classroom is what gives them value at the local level. You don't have to replace your current assessment system with badges. Open Badges are a very useful as ways to encourage a growth mindset and resilience by rewarding effort and process. Moodle gives you a simple way to issue badges in line with the Open Badges Industry standards. The student takes full ownership of this badge when they export it to their backpack.

In the next chapter, you will see examples of rubrics as a leveling up system and how the Moodle gradebook can be configured as an exponential point scoring system.

Plugin: Social Wall Format

The Moodle Social Wall will transform your Moodle course into a social learning platform. This includes a familiar post interface, timeline of posts, filtering of the timeline, and integration with Moodle's activities and resources. A social learning format allows teachers to pick up the activity and begin using it right away.

7
Leveling Up (Rubrics)

Similar to games, Moodle rubrics offer learners a way to move a level up.
The learners can identify their current level and where they would like to be
at some point in the future. Rubrics demystify the criteria for assessment,
which reduces anxiety.

Allow an hour to set up a rubric.

This chapter will cover the following topics:

- Rubrics
- Gradebook
- Exponential point systems

Getting started with rubrics

A rubric, if designed well, can make the rules very clear to a learner. What do I have
to do to pass? How do I earn bonus points? Submitting work without any idea of
whether you will meet the criteria is not very motivating.

A rubric looks like a Gamification design document because each task is organized in an order and assigned a value:

Grade:						
Rhyme and Rhythm	poem does not rhyme and has no recognisable pattern *0 points*	occasional attempt at rhyme and/or rhythm but mainly unsuccessful *1 points*		student makes a fair attempt at a rhyming poem with a recognisable pattern/rythm *2 points*	very competent use of rhyme and rhythm. *3 points*	
Use of poetic language	absence of any valid use of poetic language *0 points*	occasional attempt at poetic language *1 points*		a reasonable attempt at poetic language *2 points*	competent and creative use of poetic language throughout the poem *3 points*	
Assignment criteria	does not meet the assignment criteria *0 points*	partly meets the criteria by including either alliteration or onomatopoeia or three verses *1 points*	partly meets the assignment criteria by including two out of: alliteration/onomatopoeia/ 3 verses *2 points*		fully meets the assignment criteria *3 points*	
Relevance	subject matter does not relate to water *0 points*			subject matter relates to water *1 points*		

Figure 7.1: Always start rubrics with a zero scoring item to calculate scores correctly

Look for social media groups where teachers in your subject area share exemplars and rubrics. The Adobe Education site has a very detailed rubric on digital media by Matthew Miller that addresses both process and result:

- `https://edex.adobe.com/resource/aa8-a257/`
- `http://www.rubrics4teachers.com/`
- `https://edex.adobe.com/resource/aa8-a257/`

The preceding example of a rubric on poetry has a possible score of 10. The teacher selects one box in each row to calculate the final score. In games, scores often increase exponentially. You can create a system where each row represents a level. Level one has low points, which means failure is irrelevant.

The second and third rows become increasingly important to obtain. If the total possible score is 1500, the final score will be calculated as a percentage of the result out of the total (1500). You can show the final score in the gradebook as a numeric value or you can use a custom scale. The higher numbers help to create clear divisions for a custom scale to work predictably. In the following example, you can convert the final result to a scale of *Novice 0 - 33%, Master 33 – 66%, and Expert 66 - 100%*:

- The learners will start out at the **Novice** level
- To reach **Master** level, they will need to have 500/1500
- To reach the **Expert** level, they will need 1000/1500 (either of the final two boxes will have to be selected):

Level 1 tasks (0 – 10)	0	2	5	10
Level 2 tasks (0 – 490)	0	100	200	490
Level 3 tasks (0 – 1000)	0	250	700	1000

Here is an example of using a rubric to offer flexible assessment options. The pass mark is 35 out of a total possible score of 70. This means that the learners can have a really good portfolio (40) or a combination of other items to provide enough evidence to earn over 35:

Show me—make time to demonstrate your new skill	0	2	5	10
Record a video/audio	0	5	10	20
Tell me—write an essay or blog post in your portfolio	0	10	20	40

Adding a rubric to a Moodle assignment

The following are the steps to add a rubric to a Moodle assignment:

1. Create an assignment and ensure that you are in editing mode. Under the **Grade** section, find **Grading method** and select **Rubric**. You may access the rubric from the **ADMINISTRATION** block that links to **Advanced grading as well**.

2. Select **Rubric** and start a new Rubric from scratch. There are some required settings to be entered before the Rubric is changed from draft to published state. You may see a warning that says: **Please note: the advanced grading form is not ready at the moment. Simple grading method will be used until the form has a valid status**. Just keep going for now and your rubric will be published later.

3. Fill in each criterion and assign a point value.

4. Tick the box to show the Rubric to the learner.

5. Moodle assignments can be resubmitted many times over a longer period. You can provide a midway score to each learner and then re-assess as many times as you like until the deadline. Provide feedback to the learners to explain that their score can go up only with more efforts.

Read more on Moodle docs at `https://docs.moodle.org/28/en/Rubrics`

Watch video on Rubrics: `http://youtu.be/KXavtUhDINA`

Experienced Moodlers only

For the brave, here are a few different scenarios inspired by games, which you can use in your gradebook configurations. Think about the popular games that your learners may find motivating, and you can use these as your inspiration.

XP points and skills points

You can use two top-level categories to separate rewards for ability from rewards for reputation. Try offering people karma points for participation in forums or for taking the time to rate other people's submissions. A Moodle glossary is an easy way to collect learner input and use ratings as simple peer assessment. These points will not be included in the final assessment but will act in increasing the feeling of competence and sustain motivation. Professor Dweck's research has proven that an appreciation of process and effort is much more effective than rewarding the ability. Once learners develop a growth mindset, they have more resilience and belief that they can learn. So, an XP point system may seem playful and optional but it is far from a waste of time!

Exponential scoring

You can think of your course total as being 100 points with each week ramping up in value. So you could make week 1 worth 5 points, week 2 worth 10 points, week 3 worth 20 points, and so on. Instead of calculating the values of each activity and manually making sure that they add up to 100, the Moodle gradebook uses a weighting system to do this for you. For example, in week one you can have a quiz and an assignment worth 10 points each. In the simplest mode, these would be added up to 20 points. However, if you set the category total to weigh 5 percent of the total course value, these scores will be adjusted accordingly.

Drop the lowest x, minimum, or maximum

A great way to appeal to a diverse group of learners is by providing them the options of assessment. You can set up a range of activities that will contribute to the overall score. For example, a quiz, an assignment, and a forum with ratings. This reflects each person's strength. For example, you may start with a challenge of doing independent research and writing a short essay. The class then reviews the submissions and has an informal debate on the key points in an online discussion forum with rated posts. Then, they will do a structured quiz. Through your observations, you can see that these learners demonstrate their knowledge best in different contexts: the essay, debate, or quiz. How can you set up the Moodle gradebook to reflect this?

Placing these activities within a category provides you with many options to aggregate the category total. You can set the gradebook category total to drop the lowest score. This means that only the best two of the three activities will be retained. The other activity becomes a low-risk optional practice activity.

Another option can be to keep the maximum score of any of the activities in the category (which, in this case, drops the two lowest scores). In the case where every activity must be completed successfully, set **Category total** to **Keep the lowest score,** so if the person fails ANY activity, this is the score that is recorded as the category total. This works well in vocational competency-based systems that require every task to be satisfactorily completed.

The following images show how the gradebook category aggregation is both efficient and flexible:

Grade item	Grade	Range	Percentage
Moodle for Gamification of the Learning Journey			
Week 1			
Online Discussion Forum	6.00	0-10	60.00 %
Group Description and Icon	4.00	0-10	40.00 %
Sample Quiz	7.00	0-10	70.00 %
∑Category total	17.00	0-30	56.67 %

Figure 7.2: Start with a simple addition of scores (**Sum of grades**) to understand the calculation

Grade item	Grade	Range	Percentage
Moodle for Gamification of the Learning Journey			
Week 1			
Online Discussion Forum	6.00	0-10	60.00 %
Group Description and Icon	2.00	0-10	20.00 %
Sample Quiz	9.00	0-10	90.00 %
∑Category total	15.00	0-20	75.00 %

Figure 7.3: Drop the lowest and then Sum of grades (75%) 15/20

Grade item	Grade	Range	Percentage
Moodle for Gamification of the Learning Journey			
Week 1			
Online Discussion Forum	6.00	0-10	60.00 %
Group Description and Icon	2.00	0-10	20.00 %
Sample Quiz	9.00	0-10	90.00 %
x̄Category total	11.33	0-20	56.67 %

Figure 7.4: Average (mean) of grades (56.67%) 11.33/20

Grade item	Grade	Range	Percentage
Moodle for Gamification of the Learning Journey			
Week 1			
Online Discussion Forum	6.00	0-10	60.00 %
Group Description and Icon	2.00	0-10	20.00 %
Sample Quiz	9.00	0-10	90.00 %
Category total	**6.00**	**0-30**	**20.00 %**

7.5: Keep the lowest score (20%) or 2/10 converts to 6/30

Grade item	Grade	Range	Percentage
Moodle for Gamification of the Learning Journey			
Week 1			
Online Discussion Forum	6.00	0-10	60.00 %
Group Description and Icon	2.00	0-10	20.00 %
Sample Quiz	9.00	0-10	90.00 %
Category total	**27.00**	**0-30**	**90.00 %**

7.6: Keep the highest (90%) 27/30

Apply a scale to **Category total** and **Course total** to reward progress using game-like terminology. You can have multiple scales but only one **Letters** (unequal divisions) customization per course. You can start with a spreadsheet until you have a clear idea of the basic math behind this, and then you can search for a Moodle gradebook configuration that will achieve this. Rest assured that anything is possible!

Summary

Rubrics are much more powerful than marking guides and simple grading. Take time to get the wording correct and reflect a learner's growing ability. Personally, I can see that my relationship with my learners changes when I take the time to set up "the system" as the judge. (Even though, I am the course designer and I am "the system"). By me committing to a rule and having to enforce it, I lose my authoritarian status. Taking the mystery away from how I mark, reduces my (perceived) power.

Fairness has been my biggest lesson since using Gamification with a class of mainly young men. I have become more aware of my own inconsistencies and how generously my class tolerates my moods on different days. For example, is it fair if I don't make any comments about some students, especially the mature age students, being 5 minutes late from their lunch break? Once this was pointed out to me, I really had to think about the way I use my authority.

If a conscientious learner is occasionally late, I intuitively respond differently from how I would respond to students who constantly arrive late. So I need to articulate the rules upfront and stick to them. I could have negotiated a class rule that once a student has reached a certain level of dedication, they earn three "get out of jail" free passes, which entitle them to be occasionally late. Or better still, ask the group to nominate one person who deserves this pass during the weekly class discussion (less work for me). There is a change in the power balance if rules are negotiated upfront and agreed upon.

In the next chapter, you will see how automated reporting gives valuable insight about learner progress. In one glance, you can see who has completed the tasks and who needs assistance.

Plugin: Level Up

The Level Up Plugin offers a much quicker ways to configure moving up through levels.

Automatically captures and attributes experience points to learners' actions

Block that displays current level and progress towards next level

Report for teachers to get an overview of their learners' levels

Notifications to congratulate learners as they level up

A ladder to display the ranking of the learners

Ability to set the number of levels and the experience required to get to them

Images can be uploaded to customize for the appearance of the levels

The amount of experience points earned per event is customizable

Page to display the list of levels and a description

Experience points are earned per course

An event is fired when a learner levels up (for developers)

8
Completing the Quest (Reporting Activities)

This chapter is about using automatic reports in Moodle to show what each learner has achieved. Reporting tools help a teacher identify learners who are at the risk of not completing the course. The learners who need help are the least likely to ask.

This chapter will cover the following topics:

- Activity report
- Activity completion report
- Course participation
- Logs and statistics

Reporting on completion

When you create a Moodle activity, you have many options available to specify the criteria for what is considered 'complete'. Either the system uses these criteria to automatically tick the box or you can enable manual completion. You can use the simple **Label** Moodle activity with a checkbox to create a checklist of tasks. Learners check this box manually to indicate when they have completed an activity. If you use these completion settings, Moodle automatically creates powerful reporting tools on learner progress and completion.

Moodle also allows you to set the criteria for when an entire course is complete. Look in the **Administration** block for a link to **Course completion**. You have the choice of *any* or *all* of the requirements to be met to establish completion.

Read more on Moodle Docs at `https://docs.moodle.org/28/en/Course_completion_settings`
Video tutorial: `http://www.moodleblog.net/?p=278`

It becomes difficult to define a finish line in a large Moodle course that covers an entire qualification. Also, the course becomes difficult to navigate. There are various ways by which you can improve navigation through the use of groups, books, and lessons. Consider breaking up one large course into a dozen or so Moodle courses with a main gateway course. Using the **Course completion** settings, you can set the completion of this gateway course to require the completion of all of the other sub-courses. You can set the enrolment in this main course to cascade down to the sub-courses. This creates a central course for orientation and communication with separate Moodle courses for other topics. This approach makes Moodle courses much easier to design and use.

One of the most useful plugins to indicate both navigation and completion of activities is the progress bar which can be installed by a Moodle administrator. Add a progress bar to the default home page to visually show progress in all courses. Also, this works as a navigation tool by providing links directly to the next activity. You can add multiple progress bars to keep a track of the groups of activities or to provide advanced challenges.

Celebrating success

Think about the Moodle courses that you have seen. How does a learner know whether they have completed the course and whether they were successful? Games celebrate small and large successes. Follow the steps in your test course to add a Moodle label at the top of your course and restrict access to hide the label until the course total score is 100 percent or over the designated pass point—for example, **70%**.

1. Add a label with a message and an optional image.
2. Restrict this label by **Grade Course total > 70%**.

Remember that you can't test this unless you create a test account and enroll as a student in this course. Allow a lot of time to test your course as you have to go through each step as a student would, to be sure that it is working as expected:

Figure 8.1: Celebrate success with a label

Figure 8.2: Conditional activities can hide and show labels with images and text. Use these labels for start and finish messages

Identifying individual student progress

The reports in Moodle can be used to regularly track progress and see who is at risk of not completing. Most reports have a link at the bottom of the page to download the data into an offline spreadsheet format, which can be used for audit purposes.

The following reports are available in **Administration** block | **Reports**:

- **Activity Completion**: This grid shows all the activities for all the learners. It is, usually, only seen by the teacher but can be displayed on a data projector as a type of a leaderboard. Beware of shaming students as a motivation. I would only use a leaderboard if the scores were very close and the activities were playful, and low risk, rather than formal assessments.

- **Logs**: This filters course activity per group, learner, activity, or date.

- **Activity report**: Each learner has access to this report of their activity. This is a great way to encourage self-reflection and discuss issues with participation.

- **Participation report**: This generates a report on participation in one activity. This can be used daily to see who is on task.

- **Event monitoring**: This creates rules to be notified by e-mail when an event happens in your course. This is an advanced feature that needs to be enabled and configured in your Moodle site.

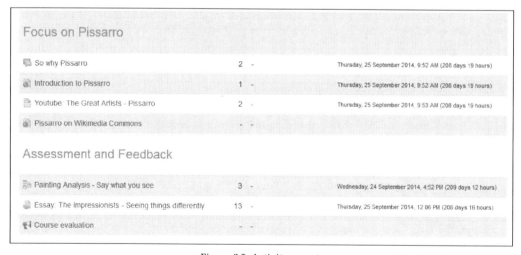

Figure 8.3: Activity report

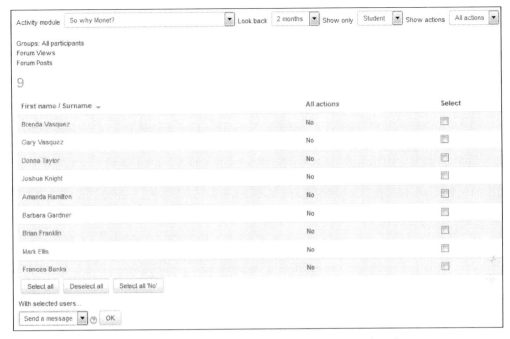

Figure 8.4: Course participation: The teacher can select names and send a message

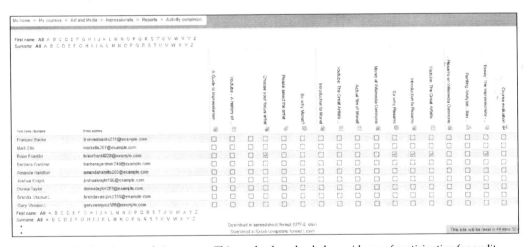

Figure 8.5: Activity completion report: This can be downloaded as evidence of participation for audit

 Read more on Moodle Docs at `https://docs.moodle.org/28/en/Course_reports`

Surveys, interactivity, and learner engagement

Over the last few years, it has become standard for most learners to have access to a smart phone, tablet, or laptop during class, and they have come to expect a whole new level of interactive media. Computer games are leading the way in this area as they are pushing the boundaries of interactive game engines, and alternate input devices (for example, Microsoft Kinect). Meanwhile, teachers are often keeping up with educational technology in their spare time as a hobby. Gamification is where the two worlds meet. Teachers may not have the budget, time, or programming skill of game designers, but they can use the game elements of Moodle to increase the interactivity in their course designs. Many Moodle courses are screen-based versions of traditional linear text books, quizzes, and exams. They have evolved from books to photocopied worksheets, e-mail and then to LMS without any fundamental change to the level of interactivity:

Figure 8.6: The average level of interactivity in educational content has not evolved, despite changes in delivery format

Moodle has an in-built survey, the COLLES survey, which measures dynamic learning practices. This is a good way to guide your course design and reflect on the level of interaction between the teacher and learners. To use the in-built survey in Moodle, navigate to **Add Activity | Survey** and then choose **COLLES Survey type**. This survey has preset questions on interactivity levels. It is added to your Moodle course for learners to complete as feedback.

If you prefer to create your own survey, use the feedback activity. This is a part of core Moodle but needs to be enabled by the Moodle administrator.

Relevance	How relevant is on-line learning to learners' professional practices?
Reflection	Does on-line learning stimulate learners' critical reflective thinking?
Interactivity	To what extent do learners engage on-line in rich educative dialogue?
Tutor Support	How well do tutors enable learners to participate in on-line learning?
Peer Support	Is sensitive and encouraging support provided on-line by fellow learners?
Interpretation	Do learners and tutors make good sense of each other's on-line communications?

Figure 8.7: Moodle has an in-built COLLES survey to measure interactivity levels

Summary

When you set up activities within Moodle, the in-built reports offer quick feedback on participation levels. This means teachers can intervene at the right time. Overall patterns reveal whether the class pace can be fast-tracked or slowed down.

If you are uploading worksheets (PDF or DOC) for learners to download, complete, and then upload again—which you then download and assess and then, upload for them to log on and check your feedback—then you and your students are probably feeling frustrated with the amount of work involved. You are probably wondering what the benefits are of using Moodle as a learning management system. You used to do this by sending e-mails with attachments and replying, so is it really any different? Moodle provides much easier ways to provide feedback and interaction. Hopefully, this book has inspired you to look for ways through which learners can directly go to Moodle and get rapid, automated, and frequent feedback:

- Checkboxes can be used to indicate the completion of tasks
- Polling using the choice activity (for both self-assessment and peer comparison)
- Forum posting and ratings
- Content is revealed to the learner as an indication of success
- Content pathways can be based on learner performance and choice

- Labels are revealed or hidden when scores are achieved
- Badges are issued to indicate success and progress
- Rubrics can be used to set clear goals

The next chapter will review each step taken so far in your test course. We will go back and add social aspects to the activities. You will see how to use Moodle groups to harness the motivational power of competition.

Plugin: Engagement Analytics

The Engagement Analytics block provides information about student progress against a range of indicators. As the name suggests, the block provides feedback on the level of "engagement" of a student. In this plugin, "engagement" refers to the activities that have been identified by current research to have an impact on student success in an online course.

9
Super-boost Gamification with Social Elements (Groups)

This chapter is about the potential to increase motivation by including social game elements in your Gamification strategies. A Gamification experiment with thousands of MOOC participants measured participation of learners in three groups: plain, game, and social. Students in the game condition had a 22.5 percent higher test score in the final test compared to students in the plain condition. Students in the social condition showed an even stronger increase of almost 40 percent compared to students in the plain condition. (See http://www.henningpohl.net/papers/Krause2015.pdf).

This chapter will cover the following topics:

- Moodle groups
- Gradebook averages
- Group averages

When implemented correctly, teamwork is a very powerful motivation. Multiplayer modes in video games are increasingly common. Team-based sports are an important part of life for many children and adults. However, tapping in to the basic human need for affiliation can be a double-edged sword. Many of us have traumatic memories of group work at school. It can be confronting, unfair, and amplify conflicts. The rare moment when a team comes together can be bliss, and these memories can stay in our minds forever.

We will now step back through everything we have covered so far in this book and add a social layer to each activity along with tips on how to use social elements effectively. The scenario presented is a digital media class where learners use a Moodle course in the classroom (14 hours) and use the course for self-directed study during out of class time (12 hours) as well. Collaboration is encouraged by small teams competing with each other. This group approach of a leaderboard with the weekly winning group, rather than individual scores, offers some anonymity and avoids shame as a motivator.

Onboarding – communication and collaboration with Moodle groups

The first interactions when joining a new class can be used to create a culture of communication and collaboration.

- Have learners update their Moodle profiles and set up communication channels
- Provide a practice exercise in using Moodle forums and peer rating
- Interact and bond with other learners to build identity
- Encourage and reward creativity and expression
- Set up peer mentoring and peer assessment
- Identify individual interests and experience
- Appoint mentors/leaders to delegate
- Establish expectation of choice, responsibility, and accountability within groups

As an orientation exercise, find a space for the class to sit and have face-to-face interactions. Briefly showcase the work produced by the learners from previous years. Ask the learners to form groups in the area they are most interested and skilled in, for example, graphic design, programming or web design. These groupings will be referred to as "Guilds" or skill-based groups. In these small groups, they can introduce themselves and discuss their favorite software, examples, and projects that they may have been involved with. You can suggest some topics for conversation if the learners are not contributing. Ask each group to nominate one or more experts to be the leader(s) for this Guild. You can adapt this in an online environment using forums or break-away rooms in a webinar.

Now ask the group to form small teams of three to five people by taking one person from each of the Guilds and ensure that there is a mix of skills. The teams are more likely to be successful if there is a mix of genders. (See `https://www.psychologytoday.com/blog/the-science-success/201104/many-heads-can-be-better-one-if-they-belong-women`.) Each group must represent a range of skills from the Guilds so that a group can have (at least) one graphic designer, programmer, and web designer (HTML). Throughout the course they will work as Guilds for some activities and in their teams for other activities. This encourages social interaction with a wider variety of people. Ask these groups to come up with a team name and an image to use as a mascot or banner based on a theme that is relevant to their group. This theme will become the basis for the Gamification narrative. A winning team will be declared at the end of the course. Some ideas for themes are:

- Sporting groups
- Novels/movies
- Lego
- Animals
- Music bands

It is important to invite learners to choose their own groups and then get to know a small number of new people in a non-confrontational way. They will develop a collective identity. Selecting an image to represent them is a way to encourage conversations, obtain insights into each member's skills, and see how the group will make decisions. This process also sets up a peer mentoring system. The people in the group will assist each other and will feel less shy about asking for guidance. Explain that they can contribute to team points only if they participate. In the digital media class scenario, the learners began encouraging each other not to miss classes or offered help with transport.

To use Moodle as a group scoring system, we will go through a few steps of making teams, setting up a collection of teams (groupings), and then change the Moodle course settings to the group mode. If you don't see these options, then a Moodle administrator will need to enable groups on the Moodle site by going to site settings then enable groups:

1. In **Administration** block under **Course administration**, select **Users | Groups**.

2. Under the **Groups** tab, select "create a new group" for each team that you need. Add people to the group.

3. Select the **Groupings** tab, and add a new grouping named `Teams`.

4. Use the little icon of people to add each group to the higher level, **Grouping**.

5. Go back to your course settings (**Administration** | Course Settings), change the **Group mode** to **Visible groups**, and select Teams as the default **Grouping**.

Groups in Moodle will take some time to get your head around and implement, but it takes still far less time than it takes to record these scores in a spreadsheet and create formulas. Once you have this basic structure in place, it is reusable for other topics and a new group of students next year. You can backup and restore this Moodle course every time you start a new class. You are building a flexible Gamification framework to plug in any amount of activities:

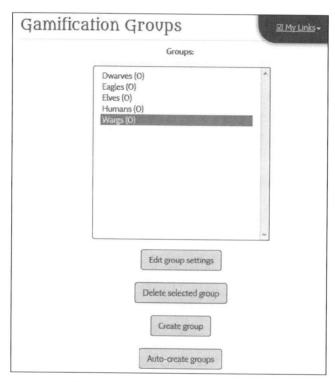

Figure 9.1: The first step is to make groups

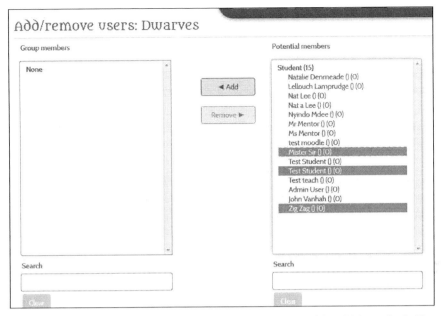

Figure 9.2: Add people to each group by selecting their names, and select Add. Hold down the Ctrl key to select multiple names

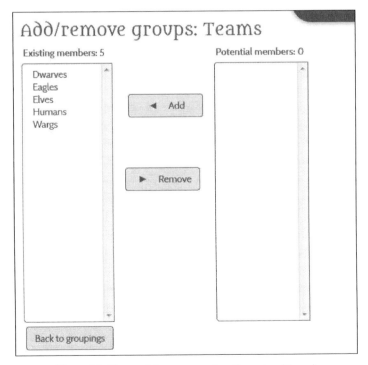

Figure 9.3: Then put these groups in a Grouping (Teams)

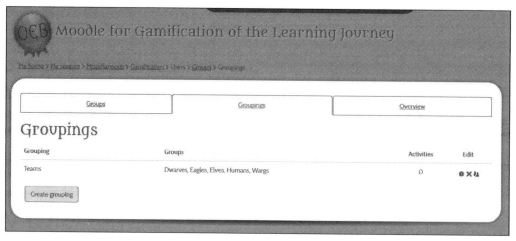

Figure 9.4: Grouping (Teams) is made of groups (Dwarves, Eagles, Elves, Humans, and Wargs)

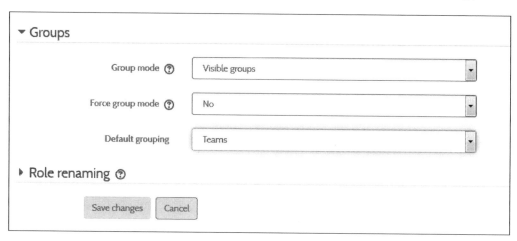

Figure 9.5: In Course settings (Administration | Course settings), change the Group mode to visible groups and select "Teams" as the default grouping

Read more on Moodle Docs at `https://docs.moodle.org/28/en/Groupings`

Group scores

Now that you have the groups set up in your Moodle course, learners can upload content on behalf of others in their team using the basic **Assignment** activity. At a mid-point of the exercise, use a data projector to show to the class the Moodle gradebook. Use the second drop-down box to filter grades by a team (group). The second last row will display the group average score for an activity. Let the learners know who the current winning team is and give them time to catch up and nudge each other to participate:

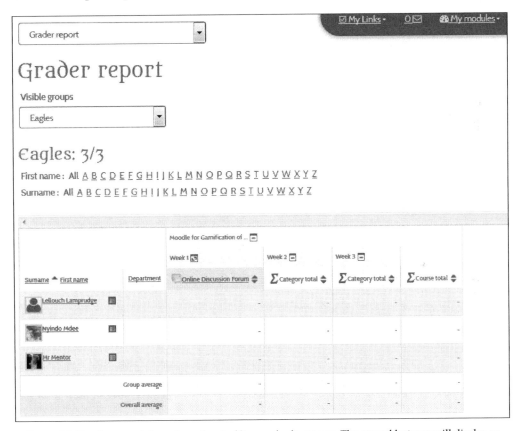

Figure 9.6: Use the second drop-down box to filter grades by a team. The second last row will display an average score for group members

From now on, every time an individual completes a task, their individual score contributes to the team total score. In *Chapter 2, Communication and Collaboration (Labels and Forums)* we had set up the forum for the learners to rate each other's profile avatar. Although these are individual ratings, they can be added up as a group average score using the group filter in the gradebook. When you try this, you will be amazed at the tribalism and collaboration a little bit of fictional competition invokes. In the digital media class scenario, the winning team was offered the privilege of sitting on a "Velvet Throne" (inspired by *Game of Thrones* and *@mrmatera* at http://www.mrmatera.com/tag/gamification/). This gave them the status of winners when in reality it was just a piece of velvet on a normal chair. The effect of this "Race to the Velvet Throne" Gamification project was immediate and resulted in higher attendance, participation, and course completions moving from around 10% up to 63%.

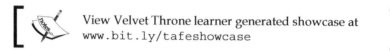

View Velvet Throne learner generated showcase at www.bit.ly/tafeshowcase

Social game elements are effective because humans are highly motivated by status. Gabe Ziccherman suggested a cascading value of **Status, Access, Power, and Stuff**—the **SAPS** model where status is more powerful than material rewards (http://www.gamification.co/gabe-zichermann/). Working with a group of learners, either online or face to face, is an ideal situation to create opportunities where learners can work towards earning status among their peers. Setting up the Guilds (with badges) is a way to provide the learners with status through various pathways and not limiting how many people can achieve the top status level; there is no individual "winner". Particularly for low confidence learners, connecting future success and career opportunities to academic achievement is not highly motivating (http://australia.teachingandlearningtoolkit.net.au/toolkit/aspiration-interventions/). A more reliable motivation trigger is status—how their peers perceive them at this point in time. In games, there are multiple scoring systems for reputation points, experience points, roles, health status, inventory, and mastery/achievement. The next time you see children playing a game, try to take that concept and imagine how you could use it to create different types of scoring systems in your class that offer status.

Challenges for learners – group submission

In *Chapter 3, Challenges for Learners (Self-Assessment and Choice)* we set up a Moodle assignment to keep scores. We used the example of the "Cup of Fate" offline activity where learners had the chance to prove that they deserve to keep an achievement award. Although you record this in Moodle as an individual activity, you can quickly collate all of these points into a group score and then calculate an average across all members of the group. You can do this by the Group filter in the gradebook to see what the average score for each group is at the end of each week. In the "Velvet Throne" Classroom Gamification project, this was how the weekly winning house was decided.

Originally, the "Race to the Velvet Throne" plan was to add up points to declare an overall winning group, but it was observed that the high achievers were banded together, so they would easily win. The solution was to wipe the slate clean each week and give every group a chance to win. The group with the most weekly wins was declared the winner.

Another issue we had was the different numbers in each group and absentees on a given day. Using this method of gradebook categories and Moodle groups automatically calculates an average score. So groups with three people were not disadvantaged against a group of five people because the points are not simply added up. Towards the end of the competition, one of the groups became so small that it was disbanded and members went up for auction to the remaining groups. That was fun!

The Moodle assignment can be used to provide a group activity by changing the assignment to group mode. The teacher decides whether each member of the group gets the same mark or an individual mark representing their contribution.

This is an example of a group activity that you can set up. Continuing from the onboarding activity of forming small groups, now ask each group to write a paragraph describing their group and then find or create a group icon/image. Assign a mark out of 10 for how well this image represents their group (or other criteria that you set). Each person in the group will get the same mark. Try this in your test course:

1. In the **Assignment** settings, tick the box to allow both online text and file upload (or **File submissions**).
2. In the **Group submission settings**, change **Learners submit in groups** to **Yes**.
3. Leave **Require all learners to submit** to **No**.

4. Change **Grouping for learner groups** to **Teams**:

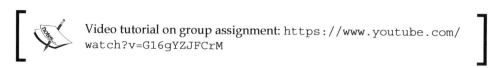

Figure 9.7: Use "Group submission settings" for group assignments. This has more options than the basic options for groups under "Common module settings"

> Video tutorial on group assignment: `https://www.youtube.com/watch?v=G16gYZJFCrM`

Ask one person from each group to upload the image selected by the group, and then add marks for the submission:

1. Open the assignment and choose **View all submissions**.

2. Enter a grade for the submission, for example, `7/10`.

3. Select **Apply grades and feedback to the group**. Now every group member will receive a mark of `7/10`.

4. Check the marks in the gradebook.

Troubleshooting groups

If attendance drops too low, consider breaking up a group or combining two groups. Using average group scores helps to even out this problem.

If members are not contributing equally, ask the group to divide the score up into percentages representing each person's contribution, or you can provide individual scores.

Use the "Cup of Fate" activity to set an expectation of rotating roles so that one person does not dominate.

Groups that encourage participation

It takes careful planning to set up group activities that encourage participation. You can set an expectation that every group member must submit an assignment and receive a grade before continuing, but this can be unfair to group members who are punished because of someone else's absence or lack of participation. I rarely use this approach. Working in a group doesn't mean 100 percent collaboration all the time. Although this is what we did in the case of the group selecting an image to represent themselves, another way is where a group can be required to collaborate on an initial concept and framework and then, work independently on their own piece before bringing it back to contribute to a larger picture. You can think of this like a jigsaw; asking a group of five people to make a 1000 piece jigsaw puzzle together and then giving everybody the same score at the end will probably end in tears or bloodshed. Or you could ask the group to choose a black and white picture and collaboratively decide on a limited color palette. You chop up the image into five jigsaw pieces and ask each person to color in their piece according to the agreed method. They are motivated to contribute to a "bigger picture" and held accountable , and scored, for their individual contribution. There is collaboration at the beginning and the end with independent work in the middle. If one or two people do not submit work, the other team members are not disadvantaged. This is an effective way of using groups to encourage collaboration because each individual is held accountable by the group to an agreed approach, yet not penalized by another learner's performance.

In *Chapter 4, Passing the Gateway (Conditional Activities)* we had set up criteria for what determines whether an activity is complete, and then we used this as a restriction for future activities. With careful planning, you can ensure that progression and the revealing of content is based on individual performance, yet you should still use the motivational power of groups.

In *Chapter 5, Feedback on Progress (Marking Guides and Scales)* we saw how marking guides can make the rules clear and offer a game-like leveling up approach. If you have 20 people starting a course on a given day, within a few days or weeks, you will see that they are all at different levels. In some areas, they may be advanced and in others, they are behind. How do games take advantage of this natural variation in performance? The online gaming world has created spaces where players communicate outside the game in forums, wikis, and YouTube channels. People make cheat guides about the games and are happy to share their knowledge with beginners. In Moodle, we can imitate these collaborative spaces gamers use to teach each other and make the most of the natural leaders and influencers in the class. The reason for setting up the Guild groups in **Week 1** was to establish a line of communication and delegation. You can quickly explain and train the most experienced in each Guild and then showcase their work to others as an example. Encourage these leaders to share their research and links on a class forum or blog. Rather than submitting individual items to the teacher for assessment, learners can create blog posts which are similar to the online version of an exercise book. Moodle Blogs are part of core Moodle and need to be enabled by a Moodle administrator. Learners can choose to share this blog with the whole world or just their Moodle site. Other learners can view what is shared and leave comments.

You can create an assignment in Moodle and then create a Moodle blog post attached to that assignment. Once the post is created, the learner can add tags and cross-reference posts to units of study.

1. Turn editing on.
2. Add block.
3. Add the blog menu. (This will not show if you are not in editing mode on a particular activity).
4. Choose the blog about this activity.

 If you prefer another blogging platform, these can be registered in Moodle so that posts from WordPress or Blogger will appear in their Moodle site blog. This method places the learner in control as the owner of the external blog, which becomes a work portfolio for potential employers.

The Guild leaders will likely be the first to meet the agreed requirements and achieve the Mentor level badges. You can then place them in charge of issuing the Master or Mentor level badges to other learners. This informal assessment is not part of their final mark but acts as a pre-assessment task. When I first tried this, I was really impressed with how well the class knew each other and how accurate they were in their assessments. They really encouraged their classmates to keep up their progress and aim for a higher level. As I had explained earlier, the criteria for each level is based on the curriculum, I could sit back and watch the class implement these standards. The process involved a lot of discussion on marking criteria and reflection on the difference between the master and mentor levels.

You may be wondering when does the teacher actually give feedback? The strategy is to use self-assessment and peer assessment and to set up "the system" as the judge so that the players/learners feel more secure about how they will be finally assessed. The teacher, as an authority figure, is the source of much anxiety and can undermine motivation when they are unpredictable. It takes a very brave learner to submit an essay without any idea of their probability of success. Even if you have never failed a test in your life, the thought of this being the first dark mark on your perfect record is extremely stressful. Peer-awarded badges increase learner confidence and motivation. By the time the teacher, as an expert, provides feedback the learner confidence is high, and they know they have the opportunity and support to resubmit to keep on improving the result.

Individual formal assessment

In the digital media class scenario, formal assessment is done through a personal blog with tags. The learners maintain a Google Blogger site with daily posts of their activities. They add labels to each post and cross reference them against the units of study. This is the basis of their formative assessment. They link the RSS (atom feed) to Moodle as an external blog so that other people in the class can see and be inspired by what they are doing.

Moodle is not used to record their academic results. It is there purely as a collaboration and motivation space to encourage and reward effort and process. The Gamification techniques proposed in this book do not have to contribute to the final grades at all. They can sit alongside your traditional marking system. You could view them as practice exercises to build up competence and confidence.

The blogs became quite large with a wide range of work showing how each person had progressed. So, at the end of the year, the digital media class set up a shared Google site with tabs where each Guild uploaded some examples of their best work as a showcase. This became the introduction for the new learners in the next year and provided exemplars of varying standards.

Summary

The aim of the preceding chapters was to provide teachers with the skills and knowledge to understand basic Gamification techniques, reduce administrative workload to free up time to be more creative, quickly identify learner progress, and provide personalized learning paths.

You now have the basic skills to use Gamification design techniques in Moodle courses that can take learners on a journey of risk, choice, surprise, delight, and transformation. Many teachers are already doing this, and in my opinion, this is Gamification. You take an activity and reframe it to be more appealing and achievable. This sounds like the job description of any teacher! Understanding games and play better can help teachers to be more effective in building learner motivation through the use of game elements.

You have learned how to configure Moodle activities to reduce teacher administrative tasks. The release from repetitive tasks will provide more time for the creative and rewarding aspects of teaching. The Moodle activities that you create will automatically create data about learner participation and competence to assist you in identifying struggling learners and plan appropriate intervention or scaffolding. The in-built reports that are available in Moodle LMS not only help you to get to know your learners faster, but they also create evidence for formative assessment, which saves you marking time.

Use the full power of an LMS by developing learning activities within the course to allow personalized learning paths. The activity restriction options in Moodle can be used to allow learners to create their own paths within the boundaries you set. An individual teacher doesn't have the time to provide frequent feedback to each person as they progress along their learning journey. Rather than creating a personalized learning path for each learner, you are using technology to collect groups of activities within which each learner can follow a different path. When the Moodle LMS is fully utilized, feedback on progress is regularly provided along the way from peers, automated reporting, and the teacher. Having learners reach the finish line at different points means that instead of spending the last few weeks marking every learner's individual work, you can focus your attention on the few people who have lagged behind and need support to meet the deadlines. The ability to set up a system that is scalable and adaptable to each learner makes it worth learning how to configure your Moodle course.

The core Moodle LMS and the plugins featured throughout this book offer many game components, mechanics, and dynamics. As described by Kevin Werbach in the Coursera MOOC on Gamification, these components include:

- **Game dynamics** — the grammar: (the hidden elements) This includes constraints, emotions, narrative, progression, and relationships
- **Game mechanics** — the verbs: The action is driven forward by challenges, chance, competition/cooperation, feedback, resource acquisition, rewards, transactions, turns, and win states
- **Game components** — the nouns: This includes achievements, avatars, badges, boss fights, collections, combat, content, unlocking, gifting, leaderboards, levels, points, quests, teams, and virtual goods

Most of these game elements are not new ideas to teachers. In fact, it would be impossible to find a classroom that is not using some of these features. It is up to you to decide which will be most effective in the current context and challenge yourself to keep on expanding your repertoire. As with professional game design, just using game elements does not ensure that people are motivated and engaged. Now you have some examples of how to strategically use Moodle activities to provide learners with choices, communication, challenges, and opportunities to create and curate content. The measure of the success of your Gamification strategy is that learners build resilience and autonomy in their own learning. When used appropriately for your learners, the potential benefits of using a Gamification Design process in Moodle are:

- Providing a manageable set of tasks by hiding and revealing content
- Making assessment criteria visible, predictable, and in plain English using marking guidelines and rubrics
- Increasing the ownership of learning paths through choice and challenges
- Building individual and group identity
- Freedom to fail and try again without negative repercussions
- Increased enjoyment (both teacher and learners)

Rather than wait for a game design company to create an awesome educational game for your topic, you can start using these same techniques in everyday activities in your classroom. This creative process will be rewarding for you and will benefit your learners because you are adapting it specifically to their needs. The system does require some preparation, but then it picks up a momentum of its own and the teacher and you will have a reduced workload in the long run. A Moodle course is a flexible Gamification platform because you are directly in control of modifying and adding a sequence of activities. Similar to other teaching activities, every time you try something new, you will see a better way of implementing it the next time. Although it may not look as good as a video game made with an extensive budget, your learners will appreciate the efforts you put in and be patient with you as you constantly improve your system. So, jump in and give it a try and enjoy your journey into Gamification in education!

Recommended reading

Books

- *For the Win* (Kevin Werbach and Dan Hunter): `http://wdp.wharton.upenn.edu/book/for-the-win/`

- *Reality is Broken* (Jane McGonigal): `http://janemcgonigal.com/my-book/`

- *The Gamification of Learning and Instruction* (Karl Kapp): `http://karlkapp.com/books/`

- *A Theory of Fun* (Raph Koster): `http://www.theoryoffun.com/`

- *How Gamification reshapes learning eBook* `http://elearningindustry.com/how-Gamification-reshapes-learning`

Index

R

reporting, on course completion
   about 83, 84
   individual student progress, identifying 86
   interactivity 89
   learner engagement 89
   success, celebrating 84
   surveys 89
rubric
   about 73-75
   adding, to Moodle assignment 75, 76
   experienced Moodlers 76
   URL 74

S

scales
   leveling up with 62, 63
scoring
   setting up, in test course 9
Social Gamification
   reference link 91
Status, Access, Power, and Stuff (SAPS)
      model 98

T

teachable moments
   creating 34, 35
test course
   scoring, setting up in 9
test environment
   setting up 8

U

User Experience (UX design) 39
User Interface (UI) 39

V

Velvet Throne learner generated showcase
   reference link 98

Thank you for buying
Gamification with Moodle

About Packt Publishing

Packt, pronounced 'packed', published its first book, *Mastering phpMyAdmin for Effective MySQL Management*, in April 2004, and subsequently continued to specialize in publishing highly focused books on specific technologies and solutions.

Our books and publications share the experiences of your fellow IT professionals in adapting and customizing today's systems, applications, and frameworks. Our solution-based books give you the knowledge and power to customize the software and technologies you're using to get the job done. Packt books are more specific and less general than the IT books you have seen in the past. Our unique business model allows us to bring you more focused information, giving you more of what you need to know, and less of what you don't.

Packt is a modern yet unique publishing company that focuses on producing quality, cutting-edge books for communities of developers, administrators, and newbies alike. For more information, please visit our website at www.packtpub.com.

About Packt Open Source

In 2010, Packt launched two new brands, Packt Open Source and Packt Enterprise, in order to continue its focus on specialization. This book is part of the Packt Open Source brand, home to books published on software built around open source licenses, and offering information to anybody from advanced developers to budding web designers. The Open Source brand also runs Packt's Open Source Royalty Scheme, by which Packt gives a royalty to each open source project about whose software a book is sold.

Writing for Packt

We welcome all inquiries from people who are interested in authoring. Book proposals should be sent to author@packtpub.com. If your book idea is still at an early stage and you would like to discuss it first before writing a formal book proposal, then please contact us; one of our commissioning editors will get in touch with you.

We're not just looking for published authors; if you have strong technical skills but no writing experience, our experienced editors can help you develop a writing career, or simply get some additional reward for your expertise.

Moodle Teaching Techniques

ISBN: 978-1-84719-284-4   Paperback: 192 pages

Creative Ways to Use Moodle for Constructing
Online Learning Solutions

1. Applying your teaching techniques through
   Moodle.

2. Creative uses for Moodle's standard features.

3. Workarounds, providing alternative solutions.

4. Abundantly illustrated with screenshots of the
   solutions you'll build.

Moodle 2.0 Course Conversion Beginner's Guide
Second Edition

ISBN: 978-1-84951-482-8   Paperback: 368 pages

A complete guide to successful learning using
Moodle 2.0

1. Move your existing course notes, worksheets,
   and resources into Moodle quickly.

2. No need to start from scratch! This book shows
   you the quickest way to start using Moodle and
   e-learning, by bringing your existing lesson
   materials into Moodle.

3. Demonstrates quick ways to improve your
   course, taking advantage of multimedia and
   collaboration.

Please check **www.PacktPub.com** for information on our titles

Designing Moodle Themes [Video]

ISBN: 978-1-78328-601-0   Duration: 02:48 hours

Effortlessly design attractive and functional themes for your Moodle course

1. Create your own Moodle skin by customizing Themes in Moodle.

2. Boost the learner experience on all platforms, from desktops to tablets and smartphones.

3. Enhance the functionality of your Moodle courses through these quick, easy-to-follow, and engaging videos.

Moodle 2.3 Multimedia [Video]

ISBN: 978-1-78216-430-2   Duration: 01:02 hours

Enhance your course and enthrall your audience using captivating multimedia

1. Create rich summary sections as well as activities for your Moodle courses using Moodle activities and external resources.

2. Learn how to create comprehensive surveys, depict statistical data in captivating charts, and use different resources to compile data as well as interactive documents.

3. Integrate several file types designed using different types of software into your Moodle courses - learn how to create and embed documents or upload them to your Moodle courses using e-portfolios.

Made in the USA
Lexington, KY
10 September 2016